The 100 Worst Mistakes in Government Contracting

Other Books by
Richard D. Lieberman

Elements of Government Contracting
(Commerce Clearing House–George
Washington University, 2004)
(with Karen R. O'Brien).

Elements of Contract Administration
(2d ed., CCH–George Washington University,
2001) (with Karen R. O'Brien).

Elements of Contract Formation
(CCH–George Washington University, 2000)
(with Karen R. O'Brien).

Government Contract Compliance:
Practical Strategies for Success
(George Washington University, 1998)
(Course Manual).

Anatomy of an Inspector General Investigation
(Federal Publications, 1994)
(Course Manual).

The 100 Worst Mistakes in Government Contracting

By Richard D. Lieberman
and Jason D. Morgan

NATIONAL CONTRACT MANAGEMENT ASSOCIATION

Table of Contents

Chapter 3. Defective Pricing and the Truth in Negotiations Act

Chapter 4. Protests

Chapter 5.   Contract Types

Chapter 6.   Multiple Award Schedule Contracts

Chapter 7.   Subcontract Management

Chapter 8. Contract Administration

Chapter 9. Contract Pricing and Costs

Chapter 10. Government Furnished Property

Chapter 11. Contract Termination

Chapter 12. Audits

Preface

This book grew out of two articles published by *Contract Management*, "10 Big Mistakes in Government Contract Administration" (December 2006) and "10 Big Mistakes in Government Contract Bidding" (January 2007). We found that one of the best ways to demonstrate "best practices" is to explain "worst practices" and the worst mistakes.

We would like to dedicate this book to our wives, Helene R. Weisz and Meghan Stewart-Morgan, both of whom are staunch supporters and helpful critics. We also dedicate this book to our government contract clients—past, present, and future: to those in the past who helped identify some of the mistakes; to those in the present who might learn from them; and to those in the future who will, we expect, come to us having discovered entirely new mistakes for the rest of us to learn by.

—Richard D. Lieberman and Jason D. Morgan

Washington, DC | September 2007

Introduction

"Wise men learn by other men's mistakes, fools by their own." —*H.G. Wells*

Although we wouldn't brand anyone who has made a mistake and learned from it "a fool," Mr. Wells does have a point. Why repeat the mistakes of others? As practitioners in the area of federal procurement law, we have at our fingertips the published decisions of the various agencies and courts that hear government contract cases. Sifting through these decisions, one finds a veritable gold mine of experience—stories of well-intentioned contractors on the road to success who took a wrong turn along the way. What is so surprising is that contractors over the years keep making the same wrong turns—the same mistakes. By looking back and reflecting on their stories, perhaps we can avoid these well-worn, yet somehow still tempting paths to failure.

This book is directed at government contractors, and it attempts to convey 100 common and dangerous mistakes so that they can be understood and avoided. The 100 outlined are drawn from every phase of the government contracts life cycle. In addition to presenting examples of these mistakes through various cases, we've also drawn from our own experience and that of our clients. Along the way, we've attempted to outline the legal framework of government contracting by providing references to the most pertinent statutes and regulations.

Although many may disagree about what should be included in the 100 worst mistakes, most knowledgeable government contractors will recognize many, if not all, of the mistakes discussed in this book. The mistakes are common and widespread. Some could be regarded as classic.

As teachers and writers in the area of government contracts, we frequently convey best practices and principles to government contractors, explain laws and regulations, and cite numerous examples of their application. Our monthly electronic newsletter (available at www.mshpc.com) is devoted to conveying such information. But sometimes reciting best practices and principles is not enough to drive the lesson home. Sometimes you have to look at the inverse. What happens when best practices and principles are not applied? Read on and find out.

Chapter 1

Solicitations

1

You failed to read the entire solicitation, including any clauses incorporated by reference.

The *Federal Acquisition Regulation* (*FAR*) requires that a solicitation include all anticipated terms and conditions that will apply to the contract.[1] Both invitations for bids (IFBs) and requests for proposals (RFPs) must be prepared using the Uniform Contract Format, which includes all terms and conditions.[2] Solicitations will also specify when you must submit your offer (bid or proposal) and how you must submit it. Read the solicitation in its entirety and follow it to the letter, even if you don't understand why or don't agree with the solicitation's approach. The written solicitation is the key to preparing your bid or proposal because it will govern your obligations and responsibilities if you win the award.

How many contractors actually read their entire solicitation before preparing their offer? Most only read the statement of work (SOW) and proceed from there. However, there are other critical sections in the solicitation that may be equally important, such as Section L, Instructions, Conditions, and Notices to Offerors; and Section M, Evaluation Factors for Award.

Here are just a few reported cases of offerors failing to read a solicitation:

- The solicitation specifically advised offerors that a one-ton truck would be needed. The offeror's failure to read or understand this provision of the solicitation did not provide a valid basis for protesting the agency's downgrading of its proposal.[3]

- The offeror should have realized that bid prices would be adjusted for prompt payment discounts of 20 days or more. Any failure to understand this fact was the result of a failure to read and apply all IFB provisions.[4]

- A protester objected that the agency failed to test a sample item provided by the protester. The protester did not submit the sample within the time frame required by the solicitation. The problem was caused primarily by the protester's failure to read the solicitation carefully.[5]

These are only a few examples of procurements where the offeror's failure to read the solicitation became part of a bid protest. But there have been many, many more cases in which offerors discovered their own mistakes or found out about them at a debriefing. Then there were no protests at all, just sad and dejected offerors that had to wait until their next opportunity to compete on a contract.

Potential government contractors must understand that many vital clauses or provisions[6] are not even printed in the solicitation. Almost every solicitation includes a provision that permits the government to incorporate clauses or provisions by reference.[7] Essentially, the government lists the *FAR* provisions and states: "This [solicitation] incorporates one or more solicitation provisions by reference, with the same force and effect as if they were given in full text.[8]" You can easily obtain the full text on the Internet, or you can ask your contracting officer (CO) for a copy. It doesn't matter whether the clauses and provisions are printed in your solicitation in full text or incorporated by reference; they will still be part of the eventual contract, and you will still be responsible for all the duties and obligations contained in them. Indeed, the typical government solicitation, which might be only 30 pages long, expands to two or three times that length once the clauses and provisions incorporated by reference are printed out.

Smart contractors print out a copy of all clauses and provisions incorporated into a solicitation by reference and insert them into the master solicitation file so they can be reviewed carefully before preparing a bid or proposal.

There is no substitute for a detailed, in-depth reading of your solicitation before preparing your offer. Only then are offerors assured that their offer conforms to the solicitation and that their prices reflect every obligation contained in the solicitation's clauses, terms, and conditions.

2

You failed to read, consider, and acknowledge all of the subsequent amendments to the solicitation.

As a matter of good business sense, contractors should ensure—for the reasons outlined in mistake number one—that they have received and considered every amendment to a solicitation before they sign and submit an offer. Contractors can easily confirm that they have all of the amendments by contacting the CO or by checking www.fedbizopps.gov, the Web site that is the government point of entry (GPE).

Additionally, when submitting a bid in response to an IFB, contractors must formally acknowledge receipt of all material amendments to the solicitation, or the bid will be deemed nonresponsive because, without such an acknowledgement, the bid does not obligate the bidder to meet the requirements of the amendments.[9] An amendment is material when it imposes legal obligations on a prospective bidder that were not contained in the original solicitation or if it would have more than a negligible effect on price, quantity, quality (specifications), or delivery.[10] An example of a nonmaterial amendment was involved in *Fort Mojave/Hummel*,[11] where the unacknowledged amendment in question would have increased the cost of a $31.4 million contract by a mere $10,000.

As a matter of practice, rather than trying to divine which amendments are material and which are not, simply acknowledge all of the amendments to a solicitation.

3

You failed to ask about a patent ambiguity in the solicitation.

Whenever you are about to submit an offer, whether in response to an IFB or an RFP, you must scour the solicitation for any obvious ambiguities. If there are any, you have a duty to obtain clarification before you bid, or the consequences may be unpleasant. An ambiguity exists when a phrase, clause, or section of a solicitation does not have one plain meaning, but has two reasonable interpretations.[12] An ambiguity may be either patent or latent. A patent ambiguity in a solicitation is one that is, on its face, glaring and obvious (for example, where two solicitation provisions clearly conflict).[13] A latent ambiguity, conversely, is not obvious on the face of the solicitation.[14]

A contractor may not rely on its own interpretation of patent ambiguities, but instead has a duty to seek clarification from the government before submitting its bid.[15] A bidder who does not inquire into a patent ambiguity assumes the risk for any unanticipated costs incurred as a result. That is not the case with a latent ambiguity. Courts will adopt a contractor's reasonable interpretation of a latent ambiguity under the *contra proferentem* rule, thus construing the ambiguity against the drafter.[16] Of course, it is the government that drafts a solicitation and against whose interest the reasonable interpretation of a latent ambiguity will be construed.[17]

The message is simple: submit your questions and requests for clarification to the CO before the closing date when offers are due. Only then will you meet your obligation to inquire, thereby ensuring that any remaining latent ambiguities will be interpreted against the government, and not against you. You should ensure that the CO actually received your inquiry by obtaining a receipt or a signature by certified mail, or from a private package delivery service. Even if a solicitation contains a cutoff date for submission of questions, the agency must clarify an ambiguity at any time before the closing date. Simply send the CO an informal agency protest with your question, and the CO must answer. A protest of a solicitation is timely at any time before the closing date. You do not need to label your letter as a protest. The Government Accountability Office (GAO) has consistently held that even if a letter to an agency does not explicitly state that it is intended to be a protest, the GAO, nevertheless, will consider it as such where it conveys an expression of dissatisfaction and includes a request for corrective action.[18]

If the CO acknowledges an ambiguity, he or she should amend the solicitation. In any event, follow the interpretation that is given by the CO in writing.

4

You relied on the verbal representations of a government official rather than on the written solicitation.

Contractors should never rely on the verbal representations of government officials, particularly during the bidding stage.[19] Verbal advice from an agency that is inconsistent with the unambiguous terms of the solicitation is not binding on the government, and offerors who rely on such advice do so at their own peril.[20]

Contractors frequently call government officials and ask for clarifications in an RFP or IFB. This is a bad practice. As previously mentioned, if there are patent ambiguities, offerors should address their questions in writing to the CO. You should get into the habit of doing and demanding everything in writing. There must be a written amendment for a change to a solicitation to be binding. The CO's verbal advice alone just won't do.

Verbal solicitations are permitted in some cases, but offerors must recognize that those situations are carefully circumscribed in the *FAR*. Verbal solicitations may be used for micropurchases, as well as those under the simplified acquisition threshold (SAT)—($100,000)—and COs are instructed to solicit quotations verbally to the maximum extent practicable.[21] Verbal RFPs are authorized when a written solicitation would delay the procurement and notice is not required.[22]

An example of the type of problem you can encounter when you rely on verbal advice can be found in the case of *Spacesaver Storage Systems, Inc.*[23] This case involved a best-value procurement for weapon storage systems, wherein the solicitation specifically provided that high-pressure laminate end panels were not permitted. Spacesaver, however, asserted that the agency had advised it verbally that high-pressure laminate end panels would be acceptable. Spacesaver's offer was deemed not acceptable by the government. Again, verbal advice that conflicts with the unambiguous terms of a solicitation is not binding on the government, and a contractor relies on such advice at its own risk.

5

You failed to request a post-award debriefing in a negotiated procurement.

Many contractors do not take advantage of the significant information they can obtain from a post-award debriefing as required by FAR 15.506 (a)(1). By simply submitting a written request to the CO within three days of receiving notification of award in a negotiated procurement, offerors can ensure that they will receive a debriefing. Those post-award debriefings are acknowledged to have reduced the number of bid protests.[24] The purpose of a debriefing is not to provide grist for a bid protest, but to furnish the basis for the selection decision and contract award.[25] Although it may come too late to help an offeror win the current contract, the information obtained in a debriefing is substantial, and may help an offeror win the *next* procurement.

In a debriefing, FAR 15.506 requires that the offeror be given, at a minimum, the following:

- The government's evaluation of the significant weaknesses or deficiencies in the offeror's proposal, if applicable;

- The overall evaluated cost or price (including unit prices) and technical rating, if applicable, of the successful offeror and the debriefed offeror;

- Past performance information on the debriefed offeror;

- The overall ranking of all offerors, when any ranking was developed by the agency during the source selection;

- A summary of the rationale for award;

- For acquisitions of commercial items, the make and model of the item to be delivered by the successful offeror; and

- Reasonable responses to relevant questions about whether source selection procedures contained in the solicitation, applicable regulations, and other applicable authorities were followed.

Of course, during a debriefing, an offeror may find out that the rules were violated and may choose to protest, but the most important benefit of debriefings is learning how to make the next procurement successful.

ENDNOTES

1. See FAR 14.201; FAR 15.203.

2. See FAR 14.201-1 for IFBs and FAR 15.204-1 for RFPs.

3. *Atl. Coast Contracting, Inc.*, B-259082, July 17, 1995, 95-2 CPD ¶ 21.

4. *Capitol Hill Blueprint Co.*, B-220354, November 13, 1985, 85-2 CPD ¶ 550.

5. *Hydraulic Design & Mfg.*, B-213756, June 5, 1984, 84-1 CPD ¶ 594.

6. There is a distinction made in the *FAR* between a "clause" and a "provision," even though the contractor is responsible for both. A clause may be found in a solicitation or the resulting contract, while provisions are exclusively used in the solicitations.

7. FAR 52.252-1 (provisions) and FAR 52.252-2 (clauses).

8. Id.

9. *Fort Mohave/Hummer*, B-296961, October 18, 2005, 2005 CPD ¶ 181.

10. Id.

11. Id.

12. *Aerospace Design & Fabrication, Inc.*, B-278896, May 4, 1998, 98-1 CPD ¶ 139.

13. See *Beacon Constr. Co. of Mass. v. United States*, 314 F.2d 501, 504 (Ct. Cl. 1963) (describing patent ambiguity as an obvious omission, inconsistency, or discrepancy of significance).

14. *Triax Pac., Inc., v. West*, 130 F.3d 1469, 1475 (Fed. Cir. 1997) (describing a latent ambiguity as [m]ore subtle than a patent ambiguity).

15. *P.R. Burke Corp. v. United States*, 277 F.3d 1346, 1355 (Fed. Cir. 2002).

16. See *Newsom v. United States*, 676 F.2d 647, 650 (Ct. Cl. 1982) (*Contra proferentem* means against the party who proffers or puts forward a thing, i.e., the drafter of the solicitation).

17. See *Salem Eng'g. & Const. Corp. v. United States*, 2 Cl. Ct. 803, 807 (1983).

18. See, e.g., *Am. Material Handling, Inc.*, B-250936, March 1, 1993, 93-1 CPD ¶ 183.

19. All invitations for bids (IFBs) require the inclusion of FAR 52.214-6, which indicates that verbal information is not binding. It states:

    > Any prospective bidder desiring an explanation or interpretation of the solicitation, drawings, specifications, etc., must request it in writing soon enough to allow a reply to reach all prospective bidders before the submission of their bids. Oral explanations or instructions given before the award of a contract will not be binding. Any information given a prospective bidder concerning a solicitation will be furnished promptly to all other prospective bidders as an amendment to the solicitation, if that information is necessary in submitting bids or if the lack of it would be prejudicial to other prospective bidders.

20. *Sw. Educ. Dev. Lab.*, B-298259, July 10, 2006, 2006 CPD ¶ 105 at *3 n.3.

21. FAR 13.106-1.

22. FAR 15.203(f).

23. B-298881, December 11, 2006, 2006 WL 3615155.

24. Steven W. Feldman, "Legal and Practical Aspects of Debriefings: Adding Value to the Procurement Process Debriefings of Unsuccessful Offerors," *Army Lawyer*, Sept., Oct. 2001; statement by Kenneth J. Oscar, assistant secretary of the Army for Research, Development, and Acquisition, before the Senate Committee on Armed Services, March 18, 1998.

25. See 10 U.S.C. § 2305(b)(5); OMV Med., Inc., B-281388, February 3, 1999, 99-1 CPD ¶ 53 n.3.

Chapter 2

Proposal Preparation and Submission

6

You failed to use the Freedom of Information Act to your benefit before formulating and submitting an offer.

The Freedom of Information Act[1] (FOIA) specifies that an executive agency must provide all identifiable records to a member of the public upon demand,[2] unless the records sought fall within one of FOIA's three law enforcement–related exclusions[3], or within one of its nine exemptions:[4]

1. Records specifically authorized by an executive order to be kept secret in the interest of national defense or foreign policy.

2. Records related solely to the internal personnel rules and practices of an agency.

3. Records specifically exempted from disclosure by statute.

4. Privileged or confidential trade secrets and commercial or financial information.

5. Interagency or intra-agency memorandums or letters that would not be available by law to a party other than an agency in litigation with the agency.

6. Personnel, medical, and other similar files, the disclosure of which would constitute an unwarranted invasion of privacy.

7. Records compiled for law enforcement purposes, but only to the extent that the production of such records would interfere with the law enforcement process or deprive a person of a fair and impartial adjudication.

8. Information contained within reports prepared by, on behalf of, or for the use of an agency regulating financial institutions.

9. Geological and geophysical information and data (including maps) concerning wells.

Before submitting their own offers, government contractors routinely make use of FOIA to gain valuable information about an incumbent contract that is up for competition—including the identity of the contractor, any prior wage claims brought by the contractor, the contract's total price, and similar data.[5] Disclosure of a government contract's unit pricing information has been a frequent source of contention, with various courts disagreeing as to the circumstances where such records constitute confidential, commercial information under § 552(b)(4) (Exemption 4 from the list) and are thus exempt from disclosure.[6]

Regardless of what is and is not exempt, you would be foolish not to use FOIA to glean as much information as possible. You can be certain that your competitors will be doing so.

7

You failed to follow the solicitation's submission instructions.

A government contractor must follow the solicitation's instructions to the letter or run the significant risk that its proposal will be downgraded. Government solicitations—especially requests for proposals (RFPs)—frequently state the exact formats required for the proposal document itself, for personnel résumés that are included, for e-mail addresses or fax numbers of past performance references, and for a variety of other important information. Sometimes the RFP can be as specific as to state that the offerors are to furnish résumés that have a font size of "11 point proportional, averaging not more than 14 characters per inch (reduction is not permitted)."[7] Page limits on proposals are frequently a problem, but you must comply with them. Indeed, the Government Accountability Office (GAO) has frequently stated that offerors are required to prepare their proposals in the format established by the solicitation or assume the risk that an agency will either not evaluate pages beyond the page limits, or will take other reasonable steps to eliminate any unfair competitive advantage that the offeror may have gained by violating the limitations.[8]

A simple and very reasonable assumption for an offeror to make is that it must comply with everything stated in the solicitation. If the solicitation asks for technical and cost proposals to be submitted in separate notebooks, do not combine them. (There are probably two separate committees—a cost evaluation committee and a technical evaluation committee—that are most likely located in two different places). If a solicitation requests five résumés, provide neither four nor six; provide five, exactly as requested. Write your proposals within the page limits. If you cannot manage this limitation, then ensure that your proposal fully "answers the mail" within the maximum number of pages permitted, and that the pages beyond the maximum can go unread without harming your proposal.

8

You failed to base your offer on the evaluation factors.

An agency must evaluate competitive proposals and must assess their qualities solely on the evaluation factors and subfactors in the solicitation.[9] When the Uniform Contract Format is used, the evaluation factors are located in Section M of the solicitation.[10] Evaluation factors and significant subfactors must be in key areas of importance and must support meaningful comparisons. All factors, significant subfactors, and their relative importance must be stated clearly in the RFP, even though the

rating method need not be disclosed; the exact weight of each factor need not be given.[11] However, the RFP must state, at a minimum, whether all evaluation factors other than cost or price, when combined, are significantly more important, significantly less important, or approximately equal to the cost or price.[12]

Contractors sometimes do not understand the evaluation factors in a negotiated procurement or the importance of internally setting up their own scheme, showing the value of those factors in the actual evaluation. (You can usually determine reasonably close percentages. For example, if technical factor A is more important than B, B is more important than C, and all three technical factors combined are approximately equal to price, the percentages would likely be 25 percent for A, 15 percent for B, and 10 percent for C, with price worth 50 percent. Even if the agency's weights are slightly different, performing this analysis will help the bidder determine the agency's priorities.) Once you determine what the factors are worth, you can then spend more time on the high-value items and less time on the low-value items. For example, if price is significantly less important than technical merit, spend substantial time developing a superior technical proposal, and devote less effort to limiting costs. If price is significantly more important than technical worth, devote considerable effort to cost reduction, while spending less time on technical merit.

One of the hallmarks of negotiated procurement is that, unlike in sealed bidding, low price will not necessarily win the award. In negotiated procurements, agency selection officials retain considerable discretion in making best-value decisions that trade cost for technical merit. Those judgments must bear a rational relationship to the evaluation factors in the RFP.[13] Awards may be made to firms that submit higher-rated, higher-cost proposals only if the decision is consistent with the evaluation criteria, and if the agency reasonably determines that the technical superiority of the higher-priced offer outweighs the cost difference.[14]

9

You failed to submit your offer on time.

The *Federal Acquisition Regulation (FAR)* states that it is an offeror's responsibility to deliver the bid or proposal to the proper place by the proper time. Late delivery generally requires rejection of the offer.[15] A bid or proposal is late if it is received at the government office designated in the solicitation after the exact time specified for the receipt.[16] This requirement seems so elementary and reasonable— until one thinks about how most contractors spend weeks putting their offers together, working on them until the last possible moment. But the law in this area is not forgiving. If your offer is late, you are just like the runner who collapses at the starting line *before* the race. There is no chance you can possibly win the award. The offer must be received on time at the place specified in the solicitation. If it is not, your offer most likely will not be considered by the agency for the procurement. Our suggestion to companies who want to ensure timely submission is simple: place one person in charge of the entire bid or proposal effort and if the offer is not submitted on time, with a receipt to prove it, consider discharging the person for failing to perform his or her job.

In extremely rare cases, a hand-carried proposal or bid that arrives late may be considered if it is received at the government installation designated for receipt of bids and was under the agency's control before the time set for receipt of bids.[17] A late offer may also be considered if improper government action is the paramount cause for the late submission, and if consideration of the offer would not compromise the integrity of the competitive procurement process.[18]

Here's an example of the highly unusual circumstances required to get an agency to consider a late bid: An agency set the closing date for proposals on Saturday. Even though the building was closed that day, agency personnel were in the building and were supposed to be listening for the expected Federal Express deliveries. When agency personnel left the building that day, they found a note stating that Federal Express had attempted delivery that morning. The agency received the late proposal at 8:28 am on the following Monday. Although the doors of the facility were locked, the agency did not post instructions for couriers on how to make deliveries. The GAO related that "[w]hen a courier attempted to enter the locked doors and received no response from within, it was reasonable for the courier to assume that delivery at that address on Saturday was not possible." The GAO concluded that "but for the agency's action here, [the] hand-carried proposal would have been delivered prior to the required closing date." Thus, the agency's action was the paramount cause of late delivery. Further, the GAO found that consideration of the late proposal did not compromise the integrity of the competitive procurement process because the proposals were not publicly opened and because the late proposal remained unopened in the possession of FedEx, where it could not be altered, after the actual closing date.[19]

There are hundreds if not thousands of bid protest cases in which disappointed offerors sought to have their late bids considered for a procurement. Most are losers. Don't put yourself in their position— make sure your company's offers arrive on time, every time.

10

You submitted a nonconforming bid or noncompliant proposal.

It is essential to submit a conforming bid in response to an invitation for bids (IFB), or a compliant proposal in response to an RFP. In sealed bidding, award may be made only to a responsible bidder whose bid conforms to the IFB and is lowest in price (including price-related factors, such as transportation).[20] Any bid that does not conform to the essential requirements of the IFB must be rejected.[21]

Examples of ways bids might not conform to solicitation requirements include the following:

- Failing to conform to the specifications in the IFB;

- Failing to conform to the delivery schedule in the IFB;

- Imposing conditions that would modify the IFB or limit the bidder's liability to the government;

- Failing to state a specific price, or stating a qualified price;

- Limiting the government's rights under any clause; or

- Failing to acknowledge a material amendment to an IFB.

In a negotiated procurement, the government makes an award to the offeror whose proposal represents the best value after evaluation in accordance with the evaluation factors provided in the solicitation.[22] One of the evaluation factors must be price.[23] A proposal that fails to conform to the material terms and conditions of the solicitation is technically unacceptable and may not form the basis for an award.[24] The material terms of a solicitation are those that affect the price, quantity, quality (specifications), or delivery of the goods or services offered.[25] Examples of technically unacceptable proposals that fail to conform to the material terms of a solicitation include proposals that do the following:

- Alter delivery locations in the RFP, or take exception to the delivery schedule,

- Add or revise terms concerning government notification as required in the RFP,

- Take exception to any specific requirement in the RFP, or

- Fail to propose a product or service that meets the minimum specifications in the RFP.

11

Your proposal contained a material misrepresentation.

Making material misrepresentations in a proposal can provide a basis for disqualifying the proposal and canceling any contract award that is based on the proposal.[26] A misrepresentation is material when the agency relied upon the misrepresentation and when it likely had a significant effect on the evaluation.[27] In fashioning an appropriate remedy, the GAO will consider the degree of negligence or intentionality associated with the offeror's misrepresentations, as well as the significance of the misrepresentation to the evaluation.[28]

Never make a misrepresentation—material or otherwise—in any communication to the government, including a proposal, a discussion question, an oral presentation, or a final proposal revision. Ensure that all written and oral statements to the government are accurate. If, despite your best efforts, you discover that you have made a misrepresentation, immediately correct it by writing to the contracting officer—regardless of the stage of the procurement.

12

In a small business set-aside, you submitted a proposal that on its face violates the limitations on subcontracting.

FAR 19.508 requires COs to place in any small business set-aside contract that is expected to exceed $100,000 the limitations on subcontracting clause at FAR 52.219-14, which states that the small business offeror or contractor agrees to perform a certain percentage of the following types of work in a contract for:

- **Services** (except construction)—At least 50 percent of the cost of contract performance incurred for personnel shall be expended for employees of the awardee.

- **Supplies** (other than procurement from a nonmanufacturer of such supplies)—The awardee shall perform work for at least 50 percent of the cost of manufacturing the supplies, not including the cost of materials.

- **General construction**—The awardee will perform at least 15 percent of the cost of the contract, not including the cost of materials, with its own employees.

- **Construction by special trade contractors**—The awardee will perform at least 25 percent of the cost of the contract, not including the cost of materials, with its own employees.

The purpose of this provision is to prevent (or at least limit) small business concerns from passing along the benefits of their small business contracts to their subcontractors.[29] Yet, occasionally, small business contractors either misunderstand the clause or are simply careless in how they construct their proposal.

In *Orincon Corp.*,[30] the protester (Orincon, a certified small business) submitted a proposal for a service contract in response to an RFP issued by the Department of the Navy as a small business set-aside. The RFP originally omitted the limitations on subcontracting clause, and Orincon submitted a proposal in which 70 percent of the labor costs would be borne by two small-business subcontractors. The Navy soon discovered its error and issued an amendment, adding the limitations on subcontracting clause. Orincon failed to modify its proposal, the Navy rejected it as unacceptable, and Orincon protested, to which the GAO responded:

> As a general matter, an agency's judgment as to whether a small business offeror will comply with the subcontracting limitation is a matter of responsibility, and the contractor's actual compliance with the provision is a matter of contract administration. However, where a proposal, on its face, should lead an agency to the conclusion that an offeror could not and would not comply with the subcontracting limitation, we have considered this to be a matter of the proposal's technical acceptability; *a proposal that fails to conform to a material term and condition of the solicitation such as the subcontracting limitation is unacceptable and may not form the basis for an award.*

> Here, it is undisputed that Orincon's proposal, on its face, showed that Orincon would not incur at least 50 percent of the personnel costs of performance with its own employees. Indeed, the protester itself admits that "the percentage of work required by the [l]imitations on [s]ubcontracting clause was not met by Orincon's proposed performance." Thus, Orincon's proposal did not offer to comply with the clause incorporated into the amended RFP. Since Orincon's proposal took exception to the RFP's mandatory subcontracting limitation, which could not be waived, Orincon's proposal was unacceptable as submitted.[31]

Note that the proposal was rejected despite the fact that more than 70 percent of the work would be performed by one small business or another. The clause requires strict adherence. In the case of a service contract, 50 percent or more of the cost must be borne by the small business submitting the proposal—anything less equals rejection and a lost opportunity.

13

In a negotiated procurement, you mistakenly expected that the government would hold discussions and provide you with the opportunity to submit a final proposal revision.

Many offerors think that they will be given a second chance to revise their initial proposal, propose a better solution, or reduce their price by submitting a final proposal revision (FPR). Unfortunately, such is not always the case. In a negotiated procurement, offerors usually are not guaranteed a chance to negotiate or revise their initial proposals by submitting an FPR. Many RFPs include a clause found at FAR 52.215-1, which states, "The [g]overnment intends to evaluate proposals and award a contract without discussions with offerors…. Therefore, the offeror's initial proposal should contain the offeror's best terms from a cost or price and technical standpoint. The [g]overnment reserves the right to conduct discussions if the [c]ontracting [o]fficer later determines them to be necessary."

Only if the CO intends to conduct discussions before making an award does the *FAR* require the use of FAR 52.215-1, Alternate 1, which states: "The [g]overnment intends to evaluate proposals and award a contract after conducting discussions with offerors whose proposals have been determined to be within the competitive range." Alternate

1 is generally used only in the more complex, high-dollar-value procurements, such as those for aircraft, ships, or complex electronics systems.

As you can see, there is no particular reason to use Alternate 1 because the basic FAR 52.215-1 clause permits the CO to have discussions and FPRs if he or she wants, or to skip them if they are unnecessary.

Although large and complex procurements— airplanes, ships, missiles, computer systems, etc.—almost always require discussions to ensure the best value for the government, many less complex procurements do not require discussions at all. Indeed, the Army, Defense Logistics Agency, General Services Administration (GSA), and most agencies that conduct procurements of commercial items have found that discussions frequently can be dispensed with, and selection and awards can be made on initial proposals.

So, heed this advice: Make sure your initial proposal complies with the requirements of the solicitation, and do your best to ensure that your proposal is competitive. You may not get a second chance.

14

You incorporated a mistake into your bid but failed to assert it.

Mistakes from which a contractor may seek relief may be either unilateral or mutual, with unilateral mistakes being the more commonly alleged of the two, but more difficult to prove.

Mutual mistakes come in two varieties: (1) a mutual mistake as to a basic assumption, or (2) a mutual mistake in the contract's integration. A mutual mistake as to a basic assumption occurs when both the contractor and the government make a mistake at the time of the contract's formation as to a basic assumption upon which the contract rested, and that had a material effect on performance of the contract (provided that the contractor did not assume the risk of the mistake.)[32] The textbook example of a mutual mistake is found in *National Presto Indus., Inc., v. United States*,[33] when both the government and the contractor labored under the mistaken belief that 105mm artillery shells could be produced using a new procedure that did not call for the use of certain, previously required equipment. After the contract was formed, the contractor discovered that the new procedure, touted by the government, simply did not work. The court found that the parties' mutual mistake as to the efficacy of the new manufacturing procedure fatally undermined the contract, and the court granted the contractor relief from the contract.

A mutual mistake in a contract's integration occurs when the written contract document fails to express the actual agreement of the contractor and the government.[34] A contractor may demonstrate the existence and terms of the actual agreement by presenting documents contemporaneous to the formation of the contract.[35]

The procedures for mistakes made in sealed bidding and negotiated procurement are the same. FAR 14.407-1 requires COs to examine all bids after they are opened to determine if there are mistakes. If a mistake is apparent or suspected, the CO must request from the bidder a verification of the bid, calling attention to the suspected mistake.

Obvious clerical mistakes in a bid may be corrected by the CO before the award and after obtaining verification from the bidder.[36] Examples of clerical mistakes include easily identifiable misplacements of decimal points (e.g., $10.49 versus $1,049.00) or clear mistakes in the unit of measure (e.g., $1.09 each versus $1.09 per case).

However, a contractor may correct more than mere clerical mistakes. Pursuant to FAR 14.407-3(a), bidders may request corrections of mistakes provided they supply clear and convincing supporting evidence that establishes both the existence of the mistake and the bid they actually intended. The agency may make a determination permitting the bidder to correct the mistake. However, if the correction would result in displacing one or more lower bids, the existence of the mistake and the bid actually intended must be ascertainable substantially from the invitation and the bid itself.

In rare circumstances, mistakes that are not apparent until after the award may also be corrected by reformation or modification of the contract to reflect what was actually intended.[37] However, reformation will not be allowed for a mistake in judgment (e.g., misreading the specifications).[38]

The elements of a unilateral mistake discovered after the award from which a contractor may seek relief are laid out in *McClure Elec. Constructors, Inc., v. Dalton*,.[39] They are:

- A mistake in fact occurred before the contract award;

- The mistake was a clear-cut clerical or mathematical error, or a misreading of the specifications, and not an error in judgment;

- Before the award, the government knew, or should have known, that a mistake had been made and, therefore, should have requested bid verification;

- The government did not request bid verification, or its request for bid verification was inadequate; and

- Proof of the intended bid is established.

A recent example of a contractor successfully seeking relief from its own mistake is provided in *Orion Tech., Inc.*[40] In *Orion*, the contractor submitted a competitive proposal for fuels management services and proposed assigning 21 people to do the work. Because of a clerical error by Orion, five positions on the second page of its manning matrix work paper were not included nor priced in its offer (i.e., its intended offer was to be based on 26 employees). The Air Force's own internal manpower estimate indicated that 25 persons, at a minimum, would be required. During discussions, the Air Force merely requested "clarifications" on personnel without specifically stating to Orion that it had failed to include the minimum manning. The other technically acceptable offer included 31 positions and was 66 percent higher in price than Orion's. The board found that these facts "should have alerted the contracting officer to suspect a mistake," and that the notice to the contractor failed to communicate the government's view that Orion's personnel plan was four positions short. Because Orion produced its original manning matrix and was able to provide clear and convincing evidence of the mistake, the board directed reformation at the price requested by the contractor.

Although unilateral mistakes are commonly alleged, contractors are rarely able to establish all of the elements necessary for relief. The law protects the government in this respect to ensure the integrity of the bidding process. Otherwise, it would be all too easy for a contractor to submit a low bid and then to seek rescission, claiming a unilateral mistake and sinking an entire solicitation in the process. Either the mistake in the bid is found not to be obvious enough to place the government on notice of the error, or the contractor cannot establish its intended bid.

Consider *Hankins Constr. Co. v. United States*,[41] when an IFB resulted in three high bids ranging from $2,446,000 to $2,298,922 and three low bids that ranged from $1,353,000 to $1,280,000. Hankins' bid of $1,280,000 was the lowest bid; accordingly, Hankins was awarded the contract, despite the bid falling below the government's estimate. Hankins soon realized it had made a grievous mistake with regard to how it formulated its bid and asserted a unilateral mistake in an attempt to have the contract reformed. Hankins argued that the cluster of high bids should have placed the government on notice of its mistake. The court found that the high bids could be explained by the industry practice of "highballing" (i.e., submitting abnormally high bids in the hope of turning a large profit but having no serious expectation of winning the contract). Concerning the cluster of low bids, the court found that the existence of two other bids of roughly the same amount tended to confirm the reliability of Hankins' bid rather than raise a suspicion about it. Regarding the fact that Hankins' bid fell below the agency's estimate, the court determined that this low bid was not unusual because in the two years preceding Hankins' bid submission, contractors had typically bid well below the government's estimate. Therefore, the government was not on notice of the mistake and had no duty to request a bid verification. Hankins was entitled to no relief.

Don't submit your bid until you have double- and triple-checked both your cost estimates and the cost estimates of your subcontractors. Although it is possible to find relief under a theory of a unilateral mistake, it is a difficult road to travel. However, contractors who discover, after award, serious errors in their bids that should have been apparent to the CO, should seek reformation of their contracts.

15

You failed to understand the legal differences between an RFQ and an IFB or an RFP, the difference between a quote and a bid or proposal, and how a unilateral offer will lapse.

In the typical situation of government contract formation, the government issues a solicitation, the contractor responds with an offer, and the government selects and signs the contractor's offer, thereby creating a binding contract. Solicitations of this sort are divided into two types: (1) IFBs in sealed bidding and (2) RFPs in a negotiated procurement. In either case, the contractor's response, be it a bid or proposal, is the offer. If accepted by the government, the response binds the contractor to perform the resulting contract.

There is a third type of government solicitation, however, which operates in an entirely different manner: a request for quotations (RFQ).[42] A contractor's response to an RFQ is merely a quote and not an offer. A quote cannot be accepted by the government to form a binding contract.[43] If the government wants to make an award based on a quote, it will issue a purchase order. However, this order is not a contract; it is an offer by the government to the contractor to buy certain supplies or services upon specified terms and conditions.[44] A contract is established only when the contractor accepts the order, which can be accomplished in two ways: (1) the supplier can issue a document stating that it accepts the government's order, or (2) the supplier can indicate acceptance either by furnishing the supplies or services ordered, or by completing enough of the work that substantial performance has occurred.[45] If the government does issue an order in response to a contractor's quote, the government may, by written notice, withdraw, amend, or cancel its offer at any time before acceptance occurs.[46]

Note the stark difference in the formation of the contract. A bid or proposal, if accepted, forms a contract. A quote, even if accepted, forms nothing. Thus, with RFQs, until the contractor receives and accepts an offer from the government, either party may walk away.

A few words of warning concerning acceptance of a purchase order by substantial performance: If the date for performance in the purchase order arrives and the contractor fails to tender complete performance, then the purchase order lapses and the contractor bears the cost of nonperformance.[47] The government will not be liable for any costs incurred.[48]

The appeal of *Rex Systems, Inc.*,[49] is a good example. Subsequent to a quote received in response to an RFQ, the government issued a purchase order for 13 rewind assemblies to be delivered to the government by May 4, 1992. Acceptance by writing was not required. However, delivery did not occur until May 14, 1992. The government returned the assemblies to Rex and denied its request for payment. Rex argued that it had substantially complied with the purchase order. The Armed Forces Board of Contract Appeals (ASBCA) rejected this contention, stating that the government had to keep its offer open only until May 4, 1992, by virtue of Rex's initiation of a substantial part of the performance. Thereafter, the offer represented by the purchase order lapsed and terminated.

Contractors have previously attempted to argue that FAR 13.302-4(b) affords them some measure of relief under similar circumstances,[50] which states: "If a purchase order that has not been accepted in writing by the contractor is to be canceled, the contracting officer shall notify the contractor in writing that the purchase order has been canceled, [and shall] request the contractor's written acceptance of the cancellation." If the contractor refuses to accept the cancellation or claims it has incurred costs as a result of beginning performance, the CO shall process a termination for convenience action. FAR 13.302-4(b) protects contractors only in situations where the government terminates a purchase order before a contractor has had an opportunity to comply with the purchase order's delivery date. Where a contractor is given the opportunity to comply with a purchase order and fails to do so, the order lapses, and the contractor bears the costs of its own lack of performance.

16

You failed to appreciate the importance of past performance in future solicitations.

Past performance information is defined as all relevant information regarding a contractor's actions under previously awarded contracts and includes, for example:

- The contractor's record of conforming to contract requirements and to standards of good workmanship;

- The contractor's record of forecasting and controlling costs;

- The contractor's adherence to contract schedules, including the administrative aspects of performance;

- The contractor's history of reasonable and cooperative behavior and its commitment to customer satisfaction; and

- The contractor's businesslike concern for the interests of its customer.[51]

A contractor's past performance must be considered in every solicitation for competitive proposals expected to exceed the simplified acquisition threshold—generally $100,000—unless the CO provides a reason that it is not an appropriate evaluation factor.[52] Because COs rarely use the exception to the rule, it is essential that every contractor take these steps:

- Maintain a database of all previously awarded government contracts;

- Retain the contact information of previous government officials, such as COs and contract specialists, who worked with the contractor on the contracts and can provide a reference as to the contractor's performance;

- Regularly check and update agency past performance databases, where applicable;

- Carefully examine all solicitations, and ensure that the requirements for submitting past performance references are fully provided; and

- Where references for past performance are submitted, follow up to ensure that the reference is, in fact, contacted by the procuring agency.

In any competition, a contractor should follow up with the CO to ensure that it receives the benefits of its best past performance evaluations. This endeavor is particularly important because a contractor cannot exercise any significant control over the way an agency evaluates its performance. For example, when offerors list past performance references in their proposals, there is no legal requirement that all past performance references be included in the agency's review of past performance.[53] An agency is required only to make a reasonable effort to contact an offeror's references. Where that effort proves unsuccessful, it is acceptable for the agency to evaluate an offeror's past performance on the basis of fewer than the maximum possible number of references that the agency could have received.[54] In fact, a single attempt to contact a reference is acceptable.[55] In sum, the GAO will not sustain a protest challenging a failure to obtain a cited reference's assessment of past performance unless the contractor can establish unusual factual circumstances amounting to a significant inequity.[56]

ENDNOTES

1.   5 U.S.C. § 552.

2.   *N.L.R.B. v. Sears, Roebuck & Co.*, 421 U.S. 132, 136 (1975) (citing 5 U.S.C. § 552(a)(3)(A)).

3.   5 U.S.C. § 552(c), providing exclusions for (1) ongoing criminal investigations where disclosure could interfere with enforcement proceedings; (2) records of informants; and (3) FBI records relating to foreign intelligence, counterintelligence, or international terrorism.

4.   See 5 U.S.C. § 552(b).

5.   See, e.g., *Instrument Control Serv., Inc.*, B-289660, April 15, 2002, 2002 CPD ¶ 66 at *3 ("[a]s [the contractor] is already aware of the prior contract's wage conformances, and as the agency has informed all offerors that the information could be obtained pursuant to the Freedom of Information Act, the fact that RFP fails to include prior wage conformances does not mean the offerors are being treated in a prejudicially unequal manner").

6.   Compare *McDonnell Douglas Corp. v. NASA*, 180 F.3d 303, 1190-91 (D.C. Cir. 2004) (holding that disclosure of prices for certain contract line items composed primarily of the costs of materials and services would likely cause the provider substantial competitive harm and were thus exempt from disclosure); with *Acumenics Res. & Tech. v. United States*, 843 F.2d 800, 805 08 (4th Cir. 1988) (holding that unit price information submitted as part of contract proposal for providing litigation support services did not fall within Exemption 4).

7.   *Client Network Servs., Inc.*, B-297994, April 28, 2006, 2006 CPD ¶ 79 at *6.

8.   See, e.g., *Coffman Specialties, Inc.*, B-284546, May 10, 2000, 2000 CPD ¶ 77 at *3.

9.   FAR 15.305(a).

10. FAR 14.201-1.

11. See FAR 15.304(d).

12. FAR 15.101-1(b)(2).

13. *Sw. Marine, Inc.*, B-265865, January 23, 1996, 96-1 CPD ¶ 56 at *7.

14. See *Nat'l Toxicology Labs., Inc.*, B-281074.2, January 11, 1999, 99-1 CPD ¶ 5.

15. FAR 14.304; FAR 15.208.

16. FAR 14.304(b)(1); FAR 15.208(b)(1).

17. FAR 14.304(b)(1)(ii); FAR 15.208(b)(1)(ii).

18. *Cadell Constr. Co., Inc.*, B-280405, August 24, 1998, 98-2 CPD ¶ 50 at *5.

19. See *Hospital Klean of Texas, Inc.*, B-295836, April 18, 2005, 2005 CPD ¶ 185.

20. FAR 14.408-1(a).

21. FAR 14.404-2(a).

22. FAR 15.303(b)(4),(6).

23. 41 U.S.C. 253a(c)(1)(B); FAR 15.304(c)(1).

24. *Marshall-Putnam Soil and Water Conservation Dist.*, B-289949, May 29, 2002, 2002 CPD ¶ 90 at *4.

25. See *Seaboard Elecs. Co.*, B-237352, January 26, 1990, 90-1 CPD ¶ 115 at *3.

26. *Johnson Controls Sec. Sys.*, B-296490, Aug. 29, 2005 (unpublished) at *4.

27. Id.

28. Id. at *10.

29. See *Transatlantic Lines LLC v. United States*, 68 Fed. Cl. 48 at 52 (2005).

30. B-276704, July 18, 1997, 97-2 CPD ¶ 26.

31. Id.

32. See Restatement (Second) of Contracts § 152.

33. 167 Ct. Cl. 749 (1964).

34. See Restatement (Second) of Contracts § 155.

35. See, e.g., *Transportes Especiales de Automoviles, S.A.*, ASBCA No. 43851, 93-2 BCA 25,745 (the written agreement omitted certain details from a price adjustment clause that were contained in negotiation documents).

36. FAR 14.407-2.

37. FAR 14.407-4.

38. *Liebherr Crane Corp. v. United States*, 810 F.2d 1153, 1157 (Fed Cir. 1987).

39. 132 F.3d 709, 711 (Fed. Cir. 1997).

40. ASBCA No. 54608, 06-1 BCA ¶ 33,266.

41. 838 F.2d 1194 (Fed. Cir. 1988).

42. RFQs are primarily, but not exclusively, used for Simplified Acquisition Procedures in Part 13 of the *FAR* and for competitive ordering procedures in the Federal Supply Schedule (multiple award schedule) contracts in FAR Subpart 8.4.

43. FAR 13.004(a).

44. Id.

45. FAR 13.004(b).

46. FAR 13.004(c).

47. See *Smart Business Machines v. United States*, 72 Fed. Cl. 706, 708 (2006) [emphasis added].

48. See id.

49. ASBCA No. 45301, 93-3 BCA ¶ 26,065.

50. See *Smart Business Machines*, 72 Fed. Cl. at 708.

51. FAR 42.1501.

52. 10 U.S.C. § 2305(a)(3)(A)(i); FAR 15.304(c)(2); FAR 15.304(c)(3)(i).

53. *Advanced Data Concepts, Inc.*, B-277801.4, June 1, 1998, 98-1 CPD ¶ 145 at *7.

54. *Universal Bldg. Maint.*, B-282456, July 15, 1999, 99-2 CPD ¶ 32 at *6 n.2.

55. See, e.g., *OSI Collection Servs., Inc.*, B-286597.3, June 12, 2001, 2001 CPD ¶ 103 at *7.

56. *MCS of Tampa, Inc.*, B-288271.5, Feb. 8, 2002, 2002 CPD ¶ 52 at *4.

Chapter 3

Defective Pricing and the Truth
in Negotiations Act

17

You failed to understand what cost or pricing data encompass.

The Truth in Negotiations Act (TINA) requires that contractors furnish cost or pricing data before an agreement on price for most negotiated procurements of more than $650,000.[1] Cost or pricing data mean all facts (1) that a prudent buyer or seller would reasonably expect to significantly affect price negotiations and (2) that were available at the time the contract's price was agreed to.[2] This data must be certified as "accurate, current, and complete" by the contractor.[3] The government's purpose in obtaining such data is to determine price reasonableness or cost realism. Cost or pricing data are factual and verifiable, not judgmental. Although it may not indicate the accuracy of the prospective contractor's judgment about estimated future costs or projections, it does include the data forming the basis of the contractor's judgment.[4] It is more than mere historical accounting data. It encompasses all facts that can be reasonably expected to contribute to the soundness of future cost estimates and to the validity of determinations of costs already incurred.[5] Examples provided in FAR 2.101 include:

- Vendor quotations;

- Nonrecurring costs;

- Information on changes in production methods, and in production or purchasing volume;

- Data supporting projections of business prospects, and objectives and related operations costs;

- Unit-cost trends such as those associated with labor efficiency;

- Make-or-buy decisions;

- Estimated resources to attain business goals; and

- Information on management decisions that could have a significant bearing on cost.

The most important aspect is that cost or pricing data is factual and verifiable. Cost or pricing data does not include statements of the contractor's judgment, but does include the data that formed the basis of the contractor's judgment. And, as noted in the definition, data includes all the facts that can reasonably be expected to contribute to sound cost estimates. If a CO requests data that doesn't meet the definition, contractors are well within their rights to state that the item requested is not cost or pricing data.

A good example of the difference between what is and is not cost or pricing data can be found in the case of *Litton Systems, Inc., Amecom Division*.[6] The government contended that Litton had defectively priced a contract for aircraft spares because it had never furnished an estimated standard labor hours (ESLH) report, which the government alleged was cost or pricing data, but Litton stated was not. Upon examination, the board found that Litton had supplied to the government all of its actual costs of manufacturing the spares before the price agreement. The board noted that in the ESLH report, Litton estimated basic manufacturing cost on the bases of standard labor hours with adjustments. The standard labor hours were based on standards for all production operations in fabrication and assembly, which were derived from engineering drawings prepared by an industrial engineer who used estimates and judgments in preparing assembly instructions. Standards for product test labor were estimated by Litton's test engineers and entered directly into a computer terminal. The board noted that "[s]ince judgments differ, no two industrial engineers will estimate the same time for any given task or, in some cases, agree on the frequency of a particular operation. Similarly, as judgments differ, no two test engineers will always agree on the hours required for a particular testing function or task." Therefore, the Armed Services Board of Contract Appeals (ASBCA) found no verifiable, auditable facts in the ESLH report, concluding that they were not cost or pricing data and did not need to be disclosed to the government.

The consequences of failing to provide accurate, current, and complete cost or pricing data may be substantial. Some examples of successful defective pricing claims against government contractors include $10.7 million in defective pricing in the case of *United Techs. Corp.*,[7] and $8 million in defective pricing in the case of *AM Gen. Corp.*[8]

Occasionally, contractors successfully defend government claims of defective pricing such as in *Wynne v. United Techs. Corp.*,[9] a case involving assertions of defective pricing on F-15 and F-16 fighter engines. After more than 10 years of litigation, the Federal Circuit Court held that there had been no defective pricing because from 1986 to 1990, the government did not exercise its contract options under the same terms and conditions contained within the best and final offer (BAFO), but instead sought more advantageous offers from United Technologies and a competitor each year. For each of those years, the CO stated in a memorandum that United Technology's revised offer was "the most fair and reasonable" on the basis of "a market test between the competitors." The CO did not review the BAFO's admittedly defective cost or pricing data at any time. Instead, the CO relied on other reviews that did not incorporate the defective cost or pricing data either.

The court held that "competitive forces, rather than the 1983 BAFO cost or pricing data, were relied upon to make the awards and to exercise the options for additional purchases for FYs 86–90," so that the government "failed to show that appellant's

defective data caused an increase in the contract price for these years." Thus, the government could not recover on any of its defective pricing claims because it failed to establish reliance on the defective cost or pricing data to its detriment.

Luck and a novel legal defense saved United Technologies in *Wynne*. Unless the contractor provides accurate, current, and complete cost or pricing data, or the data is defective. If the contractor furnishes defective data, there is a rebuttable presumption that the defective data resulted in "an overstated negotiated contract price...for it is reasonable to assume that the government negotiators relied upon the data supplied by the contractor and that [this] data affected the negotiations."[10] In the vast majority of cases, the government does rely on cost or pricing data submitted by contractors. Therefore, a smart government contractor ensures that all cost or pricing data is provided when required and that the data is accurate, current, and complete.

18

You failed to assert that the contracting officer had no right to obtain your cost or pricing data.

Aside from the issue of whether the data sought is or is not cost or pricing data, COs have a right to request only cost or pricing data in certain procurements, namely those that will result in a contract or subcontract[11] using procedures other than sealed bidding that exceed $650,000 in value.[12] Where COs have the right to request cost or pricing data, they must do so before the contract is awarded, unless one of the following exceptions applies:

- There is adequate price competition;[13]

- The contract involves the acquisition of a commercial item, generally meaning a product of a type that could easily be privately acquired in the marketplace (e.g., office supplies);[14]

- Prices were set by law or regulation;[15] or

- The head of the procuring agency provides a written justification for why the requirement should be waived.[16]

The theory with regard to the first two exceptions is that the marketplace, through competition, has already ensured a reasonable price for the government. The third exception, where applicable, renders the government's concern moot—the government has set the price of the product, thus the contractor's costs are irrelevant. The last exception is an extremely rare occurrence.

If you believe that you meet one of the exceptions, you should specifically request that the CO obtain "other than cost or pricing data" in lieu of cost or pricing data. The phrase "other than cost or pricing data" is significantly less onerous on the contractor and is described as "appropriate information on the prices at which the same item or similar items have previously been sold, [and are] adequate for determining the reasonableness of the price."[17] Examples include commercial catalog prices, relevant market quotations, and prices charged other customers under similar circumstances.[18]

19

You failed to provide accurate, current, and complete cost or pricing data to the government.

Cost or pricing data is used to determine price reasonableness of an offer. TINA states that "[a] person required, as an offeror, contractor, or subcontractor, to submit cost or pricing data… shall be required to certify that, to the best of the person's knowledge and belief, the cost or pricing data submitted are accurate, complete, and current."[19] Stated another way, the words "accurate, current, and complete" are a simple way of advising the contractor that everything required must be produced, must be up to date, and must be truthful—anything less is defective cost or pricing data and will likely result in the defective pricing of a contract.[20]

What happens if you submit defective data? The law specifically provides for price reductions, and these reductions are implemented through various contract clauses. To elaborate, 10 U.S.C. § 2306a(e) states:

> A prime contract (or change or modification to a prime contract) under which a certificate…is required shall contain a provision that the price of the contract to the United States, including profit or fee, shall be adjusted to exclude any significant amount by which it may be determined by the head of the agency that such price was increased because the contractor (or any subcontractor required to make available such a certificate) submitted defective cost or pricing data.

This section of the law is implemented primarily through FAR 52.215-10 (Price Reduction for Defective Cost or Pricing Data) and FAR 52.215-11 (Price Reduction for Defective Cost or Pricing Data—Modifications), which are the defective pricing clauses.

If the government proves that the contractor has failed to fully disclose its cost or pricing data, a rebuttable presumption forms that the "natural and probable consequence" of such nondisclosure was an overstated contract price negotiated by the parties.[21] Where this presumption stands, the defective pricing clauses allow the government to retroactively demand refunds from the contractor.

The resulting price reduction or refund is usually significant. In addition, submitting false or incomplete data can lead to criminal prosecution.

When faced with a government defective pricing claim, the contractor's only defenses are the following:

- The data in question was not cost or pricing data;

- The data in question was not reasonably available to it;

- The data in question was actually submitted to the government, or notice of the data was given to the government;

- The government did not rely on the submitted data and would not have relied on that data, even if the data had been disclosed;

- The government never advised the offeror about data the contracting office knew was defective, yet the government seeks a price reduction for that same data; or

- The undisclosed data would not have resulted in a price increase; thus, the rebuttal presumption does not apply.

ENDNOTES

1. 10 U.S.C. § 2306a(a).

2. See FAR 2.101.

3. 10 U.S.C. § 2306a(a)(2).

4. FAR 2.101.

5. Id.

6. ASBCA No. 36509, 92-2 BCA ¶ 24,842.

7. *United Techs. Corp.*, ASBCA No. 43645, 98-1 BCA ¶ 29,577.

8. *AM Gen. Corp.*, ASBCA No. 48476, 99-1 BCA ¶ 30,130.

9. 463 F.3d 1261 (Fed. Cir. 2006).

10. *Sylvania Elec. Prods., Inc., v. United States*, 479 F.2d 1342, 1349 (Ct. Cl. 1973).

11. Modifications or amendments to an existing contract or subcontract that exceed the $650,000 threshold are included as well.

12. See FAR 15.403-4(a)(1).

13. FAR 15.403-1(b)(1).

14. FAR 15.403-1(b)(3); also see FAR 2.101 (defining "commercial item").

15. FAR 15.403-1(b)(2).

16. See FAR 15.403-1(b)(4); FAR 15.403-4(a)(1).

17. FAR 15.403-3(a)(1).

18. *Contract Pricing Reference Guide*, Section 3.3, Chapter 3, Volume I.

19. 10 U.S.C. § 2306a(a)(2).

20. 10 U.S.C. § 2306a (e)(1)(B) defines it as cost or pricing data which, as of the date of agreement on the price of the contract (or another date agreed upon between the parties), were inaccurate, incomplete, or noncurrent.

21. *Sylvania Elec. Prods., Inc., v. United States*, 479 F.2d 1342, 1349 (Ct. Cl. 1973).

Chapter 4

Protests

20

You submitted a protest that did not contain all the required elements, particularly a statement of how you were prejudiced by the improper agency action.

Failing to include all required elements in your protest is likely to result in dismissal at all three of the bid protest forums. The Government Accountability Office (GAO) lists the required elements of a protest in its bid protest rules at 4 C.F.R. § 21.1. The GAO requirements are that a protest should:

- Be in writing, and addressed to the GAO general counsel;

- Include the name, street address, e-mail address, telephone, and fax number of the protester;

- Be signed by the protester or its representative;

- Identify the contracting agency and the solicitation or contract number;

- Include a detailed statement of the legal and factual grounds of protest, including copies of relevant documents;

- State what law or regulation was violated;

- State how the protester was prejudiced by the agency's actions;

- State why the protester is an interested party;

- State why the protest is timely;

- Specifically request a ruling by the comptroller general;

- State the form of relief requested;

- State that a copy of the protest has been provided to the contracting officer (CO);

- Request specific documents; and

- Request a protective order or a hearing (optional).[1]

A statement of prejudice is the most frequently omitted element in any protest. Every protest, whether submitted to an agency, the GAO, or the U.S. Court of Federal Claims (COFC), must include a clear-cut statement of how the agency's improper actions prejudiced the protester, who otherwise had a substantial chance of receiving the award.[2]

21

You selected the wrong forum for your bid protest (the procuring agency, the Government Accountability Office, or the Court of Federal Claims).

There are three forums in which a contractor may bring a bid protest: (1) the procuring agency, (2) the GAO, and (3) the COFC. Each forum is discussed next.

Procuring Agency—Agency protests are relatively simple and easy to draft. They must be addressed to the CO and must do the following:

- Identify the protester,

- Give the solicitation or contract number,

- State the grounds for the protest (including a statement outlining the resulting prejudice to the protester),

- Provide copies of relevant documents,

- Request a ruling by the agency,

- State the form of relief,

- Establish that the protester is an interested party for the purpose of filing a protest, and

- Include a statement as to why the protest is timely.[3]

In an agency protest, you may request an independent review of the protest at a level above the CO.[4] If you submit a protest before a contract's award, then the agency may not award the contract until the protest is resolved, unless an agency official at a level above the CO determines in writing that an award must be made for urgent and compelling reasons, or that the award is in the best interest of the government.[5] If you protest a contract within 10 days of the contract's award, or within five days of a timely debriefing, performance of the contract will be suspended, unless, as previously mentioned, continued performance is justified, in writing, for urgent and compelling reasons, or that continued performance is in the best interest of the government.[6] Agencies are instructed to use their best efforts to resolve an agency protest within 35 days of a contractor filing a protest.[7]

The simplicity and ease of an agency protest carries with it numerous advantages, most notably contractor savings in both time and resources. Agency protests are particularly useful for pre-award protests of ambiguities or other problems contained within a solicitation. The agency protest notifies the CO of the problem and allows for immediate correction. Because the procedural formality associated with the GAO or the COFC is avoided, the solicitation can swiftly resume, which benefits both the agency and would-be offerors.

However, agency protests do carry many significant drawbacks. There is no statutory time limit on issuance of a decision (as there is in the GAO protest), merely the *Federal Acquisition Regulation's* (*FAR's*) direction for the agency to use its best efforts to resolve the matter within 35 days. In addition, although the agency may exchange relevant documents and information with the protesting contractor before its decision,[8] typically the contractor receives nothing until after the protest has been decided. Finally, although the *FAR* requires suspension of the procurement action under the circumstances discussed earlier, agencies are not compelled to inform you that they have actually suspended the procurement action, which leaves contractors in the dark.

Unfortunately, the arbiter of agency protests is either the CO or the CO's superior, both of whom have a vested interest in the CO's previous decisions and are both agents of the government. Officials in this situation may find it difficult to resolve their conflicting roles—that of government agent and that of neutral judge. Also, note the lack of adversarial proceedings which have historically provided the best chance at discovering the truth among disputed facts. Therefore, protests involving significant legal issues (evaluation of proposals, improper awards, etc.) should be filed at either the GAO or the COFC to ensure fairness and objectivity. One final note: attorneys' fees are not available in successful agency protests.

Government Accountability Office—The GAO is probably the most knowledgeable forum because it handles the vast majority of bid protests and specializes in this area of law. The GAO is required by law to issue a decision within 100 calendar days or in 65 days under the rarely used express option.[9] Protests submitted to the GAO within certain timeframes result in an automatic stay of the procurement, which prohibits award after a protest and requires the suspension of performance in previously awarded contracts, unless the head of the procuring activity finds that there are "urgent and compelling circumstances which significantly affect interests of the United States, or performance of the contract is in the best interests of the United States."[10]

Unlike an agency protest, a relatively formal adversarial procedure is used at the GAO. The GAO obtains the agency's position on each basis of protest and permits the protesting contractor to comment on the agency's report. In addition, the GAO will sometimes grant formal oral hearings at the request of either the agency or the contractor. Contractors may request relevant documents, and any proprietary material will be provided to counsel under a protective order.

There is one minor drawback to using the GAO. Technically, GAO decisions are not binding on agencies. Because of issues involving the separation of powers in our government, the GAO can only make recommendations. However, in practice, agencies follow the recommendations. Failure to follow the recommendation results in the GAO reporting the offending agency to Congress, which could result in needless negative publicity for the agency or could jeopardize the agency's future appropriations. Furthermore, regardless of the GAO's decision, contractors are not precluded from bringing the same protest before the COFC, and the court's decisions are binding. The GAO may recommend a wide variety of nonmonetary remedies, including issuing a new solicitation, precluding the exercise of contract options, terminating a contract, reopening discussions, conducting a new round of final proposals, or reevaluating proposals. And unlike agency protests, successful protesters may receive attorneys' fees and bid preparation costs.

Court of Federal Claims—Relative to the GAO, the COFC handles fewer bid protests each year. However, those they do handle are typically complex and tend to involve large sums of money. There is no automatic stay of the award as there is

at the GAO and no designated time for rendering a decision. The COFC has specific bid protest rules, and it normally holds an informal hearing on any request for a preliminary injunction to stop an award or contract performance while a protest is pending before it. The law developed under the GAO is given persuasive weight at the COFC, meaning GAO decisions are not a binding precedent, but are considered as if they were expert opinions and are usually followed in any COFC decision.

As mentioned earlier, protesters who are not successful at the GAO can and do bring their protests before the COFC. However, the opposite does not hold. If a contractor loses its protest at the COFC, it is precluded from bringing the same protest before the GAO. The COFC will review the full agency record and will consider the GAO's opinion. The COFC will sustain a protest if the agency action was arbitrary, capricious, or irrational (just as the GAO will). However, it will not follow a GAO decision that is itself arbitrary, capricious, or irrational.[11] Protests at the COFC can take six months or more before a final decision is reached. The COFC cannot award bid protest costs, but it can award the protester its bid preparation and proposal costs.[12] And, of course, a COFC decision on a protest may be appealed to the Court of Appeals for the Federal Circuit.

Comparison—An agency protest has limited utility because the protester receives little or no information; just a letter sustaining or denying its protest. Although an agency denial may then be taken to the COFC or GAO, valuable time may have been wasted in the process.

The GAO is the preferred forum for most bid protests, because it is less formal than the COFC, yet more formal than the agency protest, and it renders impartial decisions in about half the time with half the expense. It also frequently provides for the automatic stay of protested procurement actions as previously stated.

The COFC is the most formal forum, and likely the most expensive for participants, requiring the full gamut of formal pleadings and documents associated with court proceedings. The COFC is sometimes preferred in high-value procurements where extensive discovery is necessary and may be permitted.[13] Often times, the protester has simply decided that the high litigation cost associated with the formality of the COFC is worth it.

Generally speaking, the GAO is the forum of choice for most protests. It strikes a balance between formality and cost, it provides for the automatic stay of the protested procurement action, and gives a hard due date for a decision. However, agency protests and the COFC, under certain circumstances, may better meet your needs. Consult an experienced government contracts attorney when making this decision.

22

You failed to prosecute your protest vigorously.

As previously noted, there are three possible forums for a bid protest: the procuring agency, the GAO, and the COFC. It is imperative that you prosecute your bid protest vigorously and to the maximum extent allowed by the particular forum's rules. Because the COFC requires that corporate entities be represented by counsel, we'll focus our discussion on those forums where a contractor may bring a protest on his own behalf (i.e., at the agency or at the GAO). Do not construe this section as advocating the pursuit of bid protests without legal counsel. However, if for cost-benefit reasons you choose to prosecute your bid protest alone, here is some helpful advice.

At the procuring agency, you have only one opportunity to prosecute your protest and that is in the initial filing. Discovery is not allowed, nor

will you have an opportunity to comment on the CO's rebuttal to your protest. Therefore, you must present as comprehensive a protest as possible, providing every logical reason that your protest should be sustained.

At the GAO, there is a more formal process. First, there is the filing of the protest, followed by the agency's frequent motion to dismiss. If the protest is not dismissed, the agency will file its agency report, which must include all relevant documents. The protester will then have an opportunity to submit comments on the agency report and to add relevant documents of its own. Finally, there is the possibility that the GAO will grant a hearing.

At each step in the process, protesters must present their strongest cases. The protest should include alternative theories or grounds for the protest (i.e., allege every possible violation of law or regulation that could reasonably apply). The protest should be accompanied by all known documents that support the protester's cause. The protest should also enumerate all documents in the agency's possession that might bear on the issue at hand and should request that the agency disclose them. When the agency submits its agency report, the protester should examine it carefully and request any missing documents. Most important, the protester's comments on the agency report should contest the agency's opposing assertions head-on. Anything in the agency report that refutes a protest's argument that is not commented on or objected to in the protester's comments will be deemed an abandoned protest issue.[14]

In addition to commenting on the agency report, the protester should scour the report for new grounds of protest. The disclosed documents may reveal additional violations of law or regulation that might be independently protestable. To be timely, any additional protest must be submitted within 10 days of the agency report (presumably because that is when you first learned of the basis of protest). Frequently, protests based on the agency report are better defined than the original protest and are thus more likely to be sustained.

In the event that you are granted a hearing, attend it with a full set of prepared questions that will develop the record in your favor. Provide detailed comments on the hearing afterward, citing the hearing and protest record in support of your arguments.

23

You failed to consider the implications of a bid protest on your future relationship with a particular contracting office or contracting officer.

Before you submit a bid protest, it is important to consider the long-term effect of the protest. In some cases, winning a bid protest is a Pyrrhic victory,[15] because your relationship with the CO or the contracting office may turn sour for years to come, potentially costing your company in the long run. Despite federal regulations that require government business to be conducted "in a manner above reproach" and "with complete impartiality and…preferential treatment for none,"[16] contracting officials are human and suffer from the same human frailties as the rest of us. Protests criticize the manner in which COs and their teams make a procurement selection. Thus, after a bid protest, it is fairly common to see a contracting office receive the protester with a certain chill. Be it conscious or unconscious, former protesters may be evaluated more harshly or shut out entirely from future procurement opportunities. This effect is particularly acute where the former protester holds a multiple award schedule (MAS) contract alongside other contractors. For MAS contractors, FAR Part 8.4 grants COs wide latitude in deciding which contractors will receive requests for

quotations. In some circumstances, the CO need only "[survey] at least three schedule contractors through the *GSA Advantage!* online shopping service, or [review] the catalogs or price lists of at least three schedule contractors."[17] As you can see, a CO can easily exclude contractors for whom that CO holds a grudge.

Caught between the suspected illegality of the procurement at hand and the possible loss of future procurements, what is a contractor to do? First, consider a bid protest as your last resort, which is reserved for those rare instances where informal personal discussions with the CO have failed and where a serious and costly injustice has occurred.

Second, consider the long-term implications of a protest. Will you have to deal with this particular contracting office or officer again? Have you ever received a fair shake from this CO, and is there a reason to believe you will in the future? What is the dollar value of the procurement in question, and what is the strength of your position? All of these questions should be considered before filing a bid protest. The GAO has held that contractors should not be punished for lawfully pursuing their rights under the law through claims and protests.[18] However, this ruling doesn't prevent COs from prejudicing your company in ways that are not actionable.

Third, if you decide that a bid protest is required, conduct yourself and the protest in a civil and professional manner. In subsequent hearings or submissions, avoid needless inflammatory remarks. Criticize the improper act, not the person. Civil and professional behavior should mitigate the likelihood and gravity of future reprisals.

ENDNOTES

1. 4 C.F.R. Part 21.

2. See, e.g., *Galen Med. Assoc. v. United States*, 369 F.3d 1324, 1331 (Fed. Cir. 2004) (Plaintiff must show prejudicial violation of a statute or regulation in a bid protest and show there was a substantial chance it would have received an award but for that error), and *Liquidity Svcs., Inc.*, B-294053, Aug. 18, 2004, 2005 CPD ¶ 130 at *7 (Competitive prejudice is an essential element of every protest; where the record does not show that the protester would have a reasonable chance of receiving an award but for agency actions, GAO will not sustain a protest).

3. FAR 33.103(d)(2),(3).

4. FAR 33.103(d)(4).

5. FAR 33.103(f)(1).

6. FAR 33.103(f)(3).

7. FAR 33.103(g).

8. FAR 33.103(g).

9. 31 U.S.C. § 3554(a)(1),(2).

10. 31 U.S.C. § 3553(c).

11. See *Grunley Walsh Int'l. v. United States*, 78 Fed. Cl. 35, 39 (2007).

12. 28 U.S.C. § 1491(b)(2).

13. For instance, the COFC is the only forum where depositions are allowed.

14. See, e.g., *Uniband, Inc.*, B-289305, Feb. 8, 2002, 2002 CPD ¶ 51 at *5 n.3.

15. A Pyrrhic victory is counterproductive. Although the victor may win the battle, he loses the war. After defeating the Romans at the Battle of Asculum in central Italy in 279 BC, Pyrrhus of Epirus said, "One other such victory and we shall be undone." In that battle, the Romans had exacted a heavy price on Phyrrhus; he lost a great part of his army and leaders and had no reinforcements to call upon. Four years later Phyrrhus abandoned the Italian Peninsula to Roman control.

16. FAR 3.101-1.

17. FAR 8.405-1(c).

18. *Nova Group, Inc.*, B-282947, Sept. 15, 1999, 99-2 CPD ¶ 56 at *6. ("Absent some evidence of abuse of the contract disputes process, contracting agencies should not lower an offeror's past performance evaluation based solely on its having filed claims. Contract claims, like bid protests, constitute remedies established by statute and regulation, and firms should not be prejudiced in competing for other contracts because of their reasonable pursuit of such remedies in the past").

Chapter 5

Contract Types

24

You abused the micropurchase or simplified acquisition programs by breaking down requirements to evade the relevant thresholds (or you agreed with government contracting officials to engage in these abuses).

The government has two small-purchase procedures, both of which require substantially less competition than other procurement procedures, and are outlined in FAR Part 13. The first is micropurchases for goods under $3,000, construction under $2,000, and services under $2,500.[1] No competition whatsoever is required. The second procedure involves the simplified acquisition threshold (SAT), which is $100,000 for purchases within the United States, except in support of contingency operations.[2] When acquiring supplies valued under the SAT, yet above the micropurchase limit, contracting officers (COs) are directed to solicit at least "three sources to promote competition to the maximum extent practicable."[3]

Abuses of the micropurchase or simplified acquisition procedures occur in the following types of situations:

- The CO breaks down requirements, which otherwise would aggregate to more than $3,000 or $100,000, into several purchases that are less than the applicable threshold merely to avoid the administrative burden of using full and open competition.

- The CO uses the simplified procedures to funnel contracts below the threshold to a contractor according to the CO's personal preference, or as part of a kick-back scheme.

- The CO fails to obtain the minimum number of quotations (three) in a procurement under the SAT.

- Agency purchase card holders abuse the micropurchase threshold by purchasing items for personal use. A series of Government Accountability Office (GAO) reports detailed these abuses.[4] Some lowlights of these reports include the purchase of boats, laptop computers, a beer brewing kit, a 63" plasma television costing $8,000 that was found unused in its original box six months after being purchased, remote control helicopter items, six months' worth of long-distance phone calls and other cell phone charges, Internet pornography, $400 briefcases, cigars, sunglasses, and Lego toy robots.

25

You did not request the use of the test program for commercial items.

FAR Subpart 13.5 authorizes the use of simplified procedures for the acquisition of commercial supplies and services that cost less than $5.5 million where the CO reasonably expects that offers will include only commercial items.[5] Whenever commercial items are being acquired, both agencies and contractors are well advised to use the simplified test program procedures, which are much less burdensome. Under the program, the streamlined procedures of FAR Part 12 (Acquisition of Commercial Items) will apply, as will the simplified procedures found in FAR Part 13. These procedures—which are quite favorable to the contractor—include the following:

- Rely on the contractor's existing quality assurance systems as a substitute for government inspection and testing;[6]

- Determine the price reasonableness using customary commercial terms and conditions;[7]

- Use government financing, where it is in accordance with commercial market practice;[8]

- Have the government acquire only the technical data and rights that are customarily provided to the public with a commercial item;[9]

- Have the government acquire commercial computer software or software documentation with only the licenses that are customarily provided to the public;[10]

- Use terms and conditions that are appropriate for a particular item when it is a general commercial practice;[11]

- Do not require the use of the cost accounting standards;[12]

- Use minimal numbers of government contract clauses, which may be tailored to reflect customary commercial practices;[13]

- Have an exemption from otherwise applicable laws;[14]

- Use streamlined solicitation and evaluation procedures;[15] and

- Require that only three offerors be solicited, as in simplified acquisitions.[16]

In summary, where the procurement qualifies for treatment under FAR Subpart 13.5, a contractor should always request that it be used. It is never advisable to introduce the complexities of a government procurement where the simpler commercial procurement meets the requirements of the *FAR*.

26

You did not understand economic price adjustment factors in fixed-price, economic price adjustment contracts.

FAR 16.203 authorizes the use of fixed-price contracts with economic price adjustments. This type of contract provides for upward or downward revisions of a contract's otherwise fixed price when certain contingencies occur. These allowances mitigate a contractor's exposure to risk resulting from market fluctuations, but the allowances can also limit profit. Contractors need to understand the potential bases for an economic price adjustment, to request their inclusion in contracts where appropriate, and to exercise their rights under the clause.

Economic price adjustments are of three general types:

Adjustments that are based on established prices—Adjustments will be made on actual increases or decreases from an agreed-upon level or an otherwise established price of specific items or the contract end items.

Adjustments that are based on actual costs of labor or material—Price adjustments are based on increases or decreases in specified costs of labor or material that the contractor actually experiences during performance.

Adjustments that are based on cost indices of labor or material—Price adjustments are based on increases or decreases in labor or material cost standards, or on indices that are specifically identified in the contract, such as Bureau of Labor Statistics indices.[a]

The last type, the use of identified indices, is the most common method. Price adjustments typically are made in economic price adjustment (EPA) contracts either annually or semi-annually, but they could be made more or less frequently depending on the contract's terms. Where EPAs are allowed in a contract, it is important that a contractor pursue a price increase whenever market conditions so demand. This approach will ensure that profit margins are maximized within the framework of the contract. Conversely, contractors should note that it is possible that market conditions will dictate a price reduction, thus eliminating what would otherwise be a surplus of profit. As you can see, EPAs are a double-edged sword.

In multiple award schedule (MAS) contracts from the U.S. General Services Administration (GSA), it is especially important that contractors request EPAs. Those contracts are normally awarded for five years, with three five-year options available at the discretion of the government, meaning that the contracts could extend for up to a total of 20 years. Contractors are well-advised to update their prices using the price adjustment clause in their contract, which states:

> Price adjustments include price increases and price decreases. Adjustments will be considered as follows:
>
> a. Contractors shall submit price decreases anytime during the contract period in which they occur. Price decreases will be handled in accordance with the provisions of the Price Reduction Clause.
>
> b. Contractors may request price increases under the following conditions:
>
> 1. Increases resulting from a reissue or other modification of the [c]ontractor's commercial catalog/pricelist that was used as the basis for the contract award.

> 2. Only three increases will be considered during the contract period.
>
> 3. Increases are requested after the first 30 days of the contract period and prior to the last 60 days of the contract period.
>
> 4. At least 30 days elapse between requested increases.
>
> c. The aggregate of the increases in any contract unit price under this clause shall not exceed [normally 10 percent unless a different number is appropriate] percent of the original contract unit price. The [g]overnment reserves the right to raise this ceiling where changes in market conditions during the contract period support an increase.[18]

Any contractor who fails to take advantage of up to a 10 percent price increase three times during each five-year period of the contract may be foregoing significant profits.

27

You did not understand the rights that a contractor has in a cost-plus-incentive-fee contract.

Contractors that are performing cost-plus-incentive-fee (CPIF) contracts may have rights to an additional fee (i.e., profit), depending on how well they execute the contract. As explained at FAR 16.405-1:

> A cost-plus-incentive-fee contract is a cost-reimbursement contract that provides for an initially negotiated fee to be adjusted later by a formula [that is] based on the relationship of total allowable costs to total target costs. This contract type specifies a target cost, a target fee, minimum and maximum fees, and a fee adjustment formula. After contract

performance, the fee payable to the contractor is determined in accordance with the formula. The formula provides, within limits, for increases in fee above target fee when total allowable costs are less than target costs, and decreases in fee below target fee when total allowable costs exceed target costs.

Whereas the EPA clause discussed previously is a mechanism to mitigate a contractor's exposure to risk, the CPIF contract serves to mitigate the government's exposure to risk by incentivizing the contractor to control costs. Remember, a CPIF contract is first and foremost a cost-reimbursement contract, where the government must pay a contractor all of its allowable, reasonable, and allocable costs. Thus, the purpose of the increase or decrease in the fee is to provide an incentive for the contractor to minimize those costs.

Any contractor performing a CPIF contract should first understand what the fee adjustment formula is and how it relates to the predefined target cost. The contractor should devote significant managerial attention to keeping costs within the target limits and, if possible, perform at less than the target cost. The contractor's rights in a CPIF contract are predicated on effective cost management. Once performance below the target cost is achieved, the contractor should receive the additional fee specified in the fee adjustment formula. However, this is another provision that can cut against the contractor. If the contractor fails to keep costs at or below the target cost, some percentage of its fee or profit will be eliminated.

The following are two cases in which issues arose from CPIF contracts:

- *SCM Corp. v. United States*,[19] which held that a contractor is not entitled to payment under a CPIF contract until it allowed the CO to make a proper audit of its asserted costs.

- *Western Elec. Co., Inc.*,[20] where the board awarded the incentive fee that was based solely on the incentive provisions of the contract. In reaching this decision, the board did not consider the contract's performance requirements because they bore no relation to the incentive fee determination under the contract.

28

You failed to understand the award fee formula and evaluation criteria in your cost-plus-award-fee contract.

Because a contractor's profit depends on the award fee in a cost-plus-award-fee (CPAF) contract, a contractor must understand the award fee formula and evaluation criteria in order to manage its contract appropriately. A CPAF contract is a cost-reimbursement contract that provides for:

> [A] base amount [of fee or profit] fixed at inception of the contract and an award amount that the contractor may earn in whole or in part during performance, and that is sufficient to provide motivation for excellence in such areas as quality, timeliness, technical ingenuity, and cost-effective management. The amount of the award fee to be paid is determined by the [g]overnment's judgmental evaluation of the contractor's performance in terms of the criteria stated in the contract. This determination and the methodology for determining the award fee are unilateral decisions made solely at the discretion of the [g]overnment.[21]

CPAF contracts provide for evaluation at periodic intervals during performance so that the contractor will be informed of the quality of its performance and the areas in which improvement is expected. By making partial payments of fees that generally correspond to the evaluation periods, the government can provide an incentive for the contractor to improve poor performance, or to continue good performance.

Because the contractor's profit depends so heavily on the award fee formula, it is critical—both during the formation of the contract and during the execution of the contract—that the contractor understand the formula and its predetermined evaluation criteria. By understanding and performing in accordance with the evaluation criteria, the contractor can favorably influence any fee decision by the government, which has discretion in awarding fees beyond the minimum award fee.

The following are examples of award fee cases:

- *Northrop Grumman Corp. v. Golden*,[22] where the contract had two award fee pools but was terminated by the government for convenience. Under such circumstances, the pools must be combined and the contractor is entitled to a fee equal to the percentage of completed work, which is taken from the combined pool.

- *Burnside-Ott Aviation Training Ctr. v. Dalton*,[23] where the government included a contract provision that divested the boards of contract appeals with jurisdiction to hear a dispute concerning calculation of the award fee. The court held this provision to be void because parties cannot alter a board's review provided under the Contract Disputes Act of 1978. Thus, the award fee can always be the subject of a formal dispute.

29

You failed to understand the government's incredible range of options in requirements and indefinite delivery/indefinite quantity contracts.

The government has a considerable degree of flexibility in indefinite delivery contracts, such as requirements contracts and indefinite delivery/indefinite quantity (IDIQ) contracts, which are the two most common types of indefinite delivery contracts. Before entering into these contracts, contractors need to appreciate just how much latitude the government enjoys during the course of the contract's performance.

A requirements contract provides that for specified goods or services during a specified period related to specified activities, the government must fulfill all of its actual purchase requirements for those goods and services by placing its orders exclusively with the contractor.[24] The government must state a realistic estimated total quantity in the solicitation and resulting contract, and must accurately represent past government requirements on the basis of the most current information available.[25] A requirements contract is typically used for acquiring supplies or services when the government anticipates recurring requirements but cannot determine in advance the precise quantities of supplies or services that designated government activities will need during a definite period.[26] The government typically places purchase orders or task orders when it orders the supplies or services, and the goods are typically obtained on a fixed unit price as set in the contract.

The requirements contract essentially ensures the government a source of supply at a fixed unit cost. The rub in a requirements contract is that the government may buy nothing one year and then demand a quantity so significant the next that the contractor either must purchase supplies from another contractor to meet its obligations in a timely manner[27] or risk default. Additionally, the contract is at a fixed unit price, meaning that contractors must select a price point they can live with throughout the duration of the contract. Weighed against this risk, the contractor is at least assured that— whatever the level of demand over the period of the contract—the contractor will receive all of the business resulting from that demand.

The most common type of indefinite delivery contract is the IDIQ contract. Like requirements contracts, IDIQ contracts are used to acquire supplies or services when the exact times or quantities of future deliveries are not known at the time of contract award.[28] However, unlike requirements contracts, the IDIQ contract must contain a stated minimum quantity or dollar value of supplies or services that the government must purchase (which may not be so small as to be nominal)[29] and may also contain a maximum quantity or dollar value.[30] So long as the orders do not exceed the maximum threshold, the contractor must meet the demands of the government.[31] The contract may also specify maximum or minimum quantities that the government may order under each subsequent task or delivery order and the maximum that it may order during a specific period of time.[32] With an IDIQ contract, aside from the stated minimum quantities, the government is under no obligation to continue purchasing its supplies from the contractor.

The IDIQ contract contains many of the same risks evident in the requirements contract—uncertainty as to the level of demand and uncertainty as to whether the contractor will be able to meet that demand in a timely manner. The IDIQ contract mitigates this risk somewhat with its mandatory minimum and optional maximum ordering thresholds. However, this mitigation can serve as cold comfort, where the range between the two (assuming there is a maximum threshold) is exceptionally wide.

As you can see from the descriptions, even though a requirements or IDIQ contract can represent a significant amount of business for a contractor, there are some serious risks. Those risks make the contract vehicles less than desirable, unless contactors can accurately assess and price the risk into their contracts. Remember that declining a valid order under either type of contract is not an option without the possibility that the government will terminate the contract for default.

Two typical problems with indefinite delivery contracts are illustrated in the following two cases:

- *In White v. Delta Const. Int'l., Inc.*,[33] the court held that if the government breaches an IDIQ contract by failing to buy the specified minimum, the proper measure of damages is the profit loss suffered by the contractor, not the total amount that the contractor would have received without the breach.

- *In Rumsfeld v. Applied Cos, Inc.*,[34] the government breached a requirements contract by negligently failing to inform the contractor that the quantity estimates in the solicitation had been greatly overstated. The contractor was entitled to an equitable adjustment in the price of the units it delivered under the contract, but the contractor was not entitled to expectation damages (i.e., the contractor's anticipated profit under the contract).

ENDNOTES

4. FAR 2.101 (defining "micropurchase threshold").

5. FAR 2.101 (defining "simplified acquisition threshold").

6. FAR 13.104(b).

7. See *Purchase Cards, Control Weaknesses Leave DHS Highly Vulnerable to Fraudulent, Improper, and Abusive Activity*, GAO 06-957-T, Sept. 2006; *Purchase Cards, Navy Is Vulnerable to Fraud and Abuse but Is Taking Action to Resolve Control Weaknesses*, GAO-02-1041, Sept. 2002; and *Purchase Cards, Increased Management Oversight and Control Could Save Hundreds of Millions of Dollars*, GAO-04-717T, Apr. 2004.

8. FAR 13.500(a).

9. FAR 12.208.

10. FAR 12.209.

11. FAR 12.210.

12. FAR 12.211.

13. FAR 12.212.

14. FAR 12.213.

15. FAR 12.214.

16. FAR 12.301; FAR 12.302.

17. FAR 12.503; FAR 12.504; FAR 13.005.

18. FAR 12.601; FAR 12.602.

19. FAR 13.104(b).

20. FAR 16.203-1.

21. GSAM 552.216-70.

22. 645 F.2d 893 (Ct. Cl. 1981).

23. ASBCA No. 16110, 73-1 BCA ¶ 10,013.

24. FAR 16.405-2(a).

25. 136 F.3d 1479 (Fed. Cir. 1998).

26. 107 F.3d 854 (Fed. Cir. 1997).

27. See FAR 16.503.

28. FAR 16.503(a)(1).

29. FAR 16.503(b).

30. The delivery period is typically expressed as "DARO" or "delivery after receipt of order."

31. FAR 16.501-2.

32. FAR 16.504(a)(2).

33. FAR 16.504(a).

34. FAR 16.504(a)(1).

35. FAR 16.504(a)(3).

36. 285 F.3d 1040 (Fed. Cir. 2002).

37. 325 F.3d 1328 (Fed. Cir. 2003).

Chapter 6

Multiple Award Schedule Contracts

30

You failed to give most-favored-customer pricing to the government throughout the entire life of the contract.

A General Services Administration (GSA) Multiple Award Schedule (MAS), also known as a Federal Supply Schedule, provides a simplified process for obtaining commercial supplies and services at prices associated with volume buying.[1] The volume of purchases from such schedules is now more than $35 billion annually, even though GSA's volume declined as a result of the Abu Ghraib prison scandal.[2]

Many contractors believe they have reached a state of nirvana when they obtain an MAS contract. They think they now have a "license to sell" to the federal government and, therefore, a continuous source of revenue. However, some contractors are blissfully unaware of the terms and conditions in the MAS contract, particularly the price reductions clause.[3] This clause requires the contractor to reduce its prices under the MAS contract if the contractor grants more favorable terms or conditions to another. Many contractors overlook this requirement, and the discrepancy is not discovered until after an audit many years later—whereupon GSA demands huge refunds.

The solution to this problem is central control of MAS pricing by the contractor, so that any time a price reduction triggers the clause, the contractor can ensure that all future sales are made at the new, lower price.

31

You failed to fully and properly disclose your commercial sales practices on the GSA Commercial Sales Practice Form.

As part of a contractor's proposal for an MAS contract, the contractor will be required to disclose "other than cost or pricing data" in the form of its commercial sales practices.[4] Essentially, GSA provides a form that asks contractors to provide all discounts and concessions in their commercial sales. Failure to make a full and complete disclosure can result in defective pricing of contracts (see the previous discussion of defective pricing) and can expose the contractor to defective pricing refunds[5] or to an MAS price adjustment (i.e., a refund to the government) for failure to provide accurate information.[6] Either adjustment is likely to be significant, so it is important that you fully disclose your commercial sales practices. The GSA will seek all discounts and concessions that you give to commercial customers.

A discount is defined as:

> [A] reduction to catalog prices (published or unpublished). Discounts include, but are not limited to, rebates, quantity discounts, purchase option credits, and any other terms or conditions other than concessions which reduce the amount of money a customer ultimately pays for goods or services ordered or received. Any net price lower than the list price is considered a "discount" by the percentage difference from the list price to the net price.[7]

A concession is defined as:

> [A] benefit, enhancement, or privilege (other than a discount), which either reduces the overall cost of a customer's acquisition or encourages a customer to consummate a purchase. Concessions

include, but are not limited to, freight allowance, extended warranty, extended price guarantees, free installation, and bonus goods."[8]

A contractor must provide its discount and concession information to the government before the award of the MAS contract. *3M Business Prods. Sales, Inc.*,[9] is a good example. 3M received a contract for microphotographic equipment and supplies. When 3M reported to GSA on its discounts before the contract award, it did not include any sales or discount information for two classes of its commercial sales: (1) definite quantity sales contracts that exceeded the maximum ordering limitation (MOL) in the GSA contract, and (2) indefinite quantity contracts that included prices and discounts more favorable than those found in the GSA contract. The government sought substantial after-the-fact price reductions for discounts given in these areas, which were also not provided to the government per the price reductions clause.

As to the definite quantity contracts exceeding the MOL, the board held that 3M was not obliged to furnish discount information on these contracts, because the discount schedule and marketing data (DSMD) sheets contained no specific language requiring offerors to submit discount information for definite-quantity contracts above the MOL. However, 3M's indefinite quantity contracts with two of its commercial customers were another matter. The board held that because 3M failed to provide the discount and pricing information included in these contracts and offered undisclosed higher discounts to its commercial customers, the company had violated the contract pricing provisions, and the government was entitled to a price reduction under the price reductions clause.

In another case, *United States v. Data Translation, Inc.*,[10] the Court of Appeals held that the price disclosure provisions in Data Translation's MAS

contract were not sufficiently comprehensible to enforce and that no reasonable person negotiating with GSA could have believed that GSA really wanted the complete and total disclosure of all the information for which GSA's language seemed to ask. The court concluded that whatever GSA's subjective intent, its words and requests—considered objectively by a reasonable supplier in the circumstances—did not call for literal compliance. The duty of Data Translation, Inc. was to make a practical effort to supply relevant price discount data (i.e., to provide the same price discounts that the company normally provided to others making purchases roughly comparable to those made by the government through the MAS contract). Because Data Translation, Inc. met this duty, it did not engage in defective pricing, nor was there a violation of the False Claims Act.

Because most price disclosure provisions are not so ambiguous, contractors should be able to comply with them in full. Ambiguity aside, full disclosure from the beginning is the recommended and necessary course of action.

32

You failed to carefully establish the category of customer that will be used in connection with your MAS contract's price reductions clause.

Establishment of a well-chosen category of customer in the formation of your MAS contract is critical. If you select a very wide category (for example, "all commercial sales"), you will be forced to reduce prices to the government whenever that type of sale is made. This reduced pricing is triggered because the price reductions clause in the MAS contract[11] states that:

[B]efore award of a contract, the [c]ontracting [o]fficer and the [o]fferor will agree upon (1) the customer (or category of customers) which will be the basis of award, and (2) the [g]overnment's price or discount relationship to the identified customer (or category of customers). This relationship shall be maintained throughout the contract period. Any change in the [c]ontractor's commercial pricing or discount arrangement applicable to the identified customer (or category of customers) which disturbs this relationship shall constitute a price reduction.

How can you avoid a price reduction every time you provide a commercial discount or concession? Establish a category of customer that is narrowly defined, so that only particular types of sales will trigger the price reductions clause. For example, if you make sales to different sectors within the commercial marketplace, you might try to use only one sector. If you sell overseas, you might try to exclude that category of customer in your category of customer that is the basis of award.

ENDNOTES

1. See FAR Part 8.4.

2. At its heart, the Abu Ghraib scandal was in some ways a failure of the federal acquisition community. The Army improperly obtained interrogators and screeners through an MAS contract for, of all things, information technology. See GAO-05-201, "Interagency Contracting: Problems with DOD's and Interior's Orders to Support Military Operations," April 29, 2005.

3. GSAM 552.238-75.

4. The commercial sales practice (CSP) form replaced the GSA's previous form, which was known as the discount schedule and marketing data (DSMD) form. Both forms asked the offeror to report the discounts and concessions that it granted to buyers.

5. FAR 52.215-10.

6. GSAR 552.215-72.

7. GSAR 552.212-70.

8. Id.

9. GSBCA No. 4878, 78-2 BCA ¶ 13,362.

10. 984 F.2d 1256 (1st Cir. 1992).

11. GSAR 552.238-75.

Chapter 7

Subcontract Management

33

You failed to flow down your *FAR* clauses to your subcontractors and suppliers, particularly the termination for convenience and changes clauses.

Many government contracts are complex and require contractors to obtain assistance from other contractors in order to fully perform them. A common method is the use of subcontracts between the prime contractor and a subcontractor. A subcontractor is generally any firm that supplies materials or performs services for a prime contractor pursuant to the requirements of a government contract. Subcontract management is critical, and this management begins with the drafting of a proper subcontract.

Certain clauses in the government's prime contract must flow down (i.e., be incorporated into the subcontracts awarded by the prime). These clauses are designed to protect the government's interests and to promote government policies. Some clauses explicitly mandate their inclusion in all subcontracts (e.g., the audit clause,[1] the cost accounting standards clause,[2] and the equal opportunity clauses[3]), while other clauses implicitly require their flow-down (e.g., the Davis-Bacon Act[4] and the Service Contract Act of 1965 clauses[5]). Strangely enough, the government does not require, either implicitly or explicitly, the flow-down of the changes clause,[6] or the termination for convenience clause.[7] However, it is essential that these two clauses flow down in every subcontract. The concepts of a change or a termination for convenience are antithetical to the common law governing commercial contracts, which would otherwise require mutual agreement by the parties in order to change any term of an existing contract.[8] Failure to include these clauses in a subcontract will leave the prime contractor vulnerable.

Termination for Convenience—A termination for convenience typically occurs where funds to continue a contract become unavailable or there is a change in the government's requirements (e.g., there is an advance in technology or an ongoing war ends). The clause provides the government with the ability to quickly adjust to changing needs. The result is that government contractors must also provide themselves with similar flexibility in their subcontracts. Therefore, it is imperative that prime contractors reserve the right to terminate their subcontracts in the event of a government termination for convenience.

Subcontracts should state: "In the event that the prime contract is terminated in whole or in part for convenience of the government, the prime contractor may terminate performance under this subcontract to the same extent as the prime contract was terminated." This arrangement preserves the fairness and commerciality of the subcontract. The prime contractor does not enjoy the unfettered right to terminate for convenience whenever it wishes, but it retains the right to terminate for convenience if and to the extent that the government does so. Absent this right, the prime contractor would be forced to continue a subcontract even after the government has indicated it no longer wants the goods or services. By including the termination for convenience clause, the prime contractor can terminate the subcontractor, subsequently obtain a termination settlement proposal from the subcontractor, and then incorporate that subcontractor's proposal into the overall termination for convenience settlement proposal, thus protecting both the prime and subcontractors.

Changes—The changes clause provides the government the necessary flexibility to meet its changing needs. As requirements fluctuate, the government will issue a change order, thus unilaterally modifying a contract, provided the change is within the overall scope of the existing contract. Of course, contractors are entitled to an equitable adjustment in time and cost resulting from those change orders. But, again, it is essential that the changes clause be included in all subcontracts in the same manner as the termination for convenience clause. Specifically, the prime contractor should reserve the right to "make changes within the general scope of this subcontract in any one or more of the following: drawings, designs, or specifications…method of shipment…or place of delivery, to the extent the prime contract is changed by the government and this change affects the subcontract." Again, the subcontractor should be granted a right to an equitable adjustment. Absent the right to make a change in the subcontract, the prime contractor will be forced to accept goods for which specifications have changed or, more likely, goods or services that are of no use whatsoever to the prime contractor or the government because the government has issued a change order. By including the changes clause, the prime contractor can flow down any changes from the government, obtain the subcontractor's request for equitable adjustment (REA), and then incorporate that REA into the overall REA for the change order.

Aside from the termination for convenience and change clauses, prime contractors should examine their contracts carefully and, whenever there is a doubt, flow down a particular *FAR* clause to the subcontract. For instance, the termination for default clause[9] substantially restates the common law remedy of cover in the event of default (i.e., the contractor is liable to the government for the excess cost of reprocurement). Yet, no harm is caused by its inclusion in a subcontract, and it will serve to explicitly state the prime contractor's remedy in the case of a subcontractor's default.

The flow-down of *FAR* clauses is accomplished easily by incorporating the text of the clause by reference to its *FAR* number, and by stating in the subcontract that "the clauses are incorporated by reference with the same force and effect as if set forth in full text." The subcontract should go on to state that whenever the term "government or contracting officer" appears in the clause, it shall be replaced by "prime contractor" and whenever the term "contractor or prime contractor" appears in the clause, it shall be replaced by "subcontractor." Subcontracts, like prime contracts, commonly include pages of *FAR* clauses incorporated by reference. Their inclusion will protect you and your subcontractors.

34

You failed to prepare a satisfactory small business subcontracting plan, if required.

Section 8(d) of the Small Business Act[10] requires, in acquisitions for goods or services over $550,000 or construction contracts over $1 million, that the offeror submit an acceptable subcontracting plan showing how it will provide opportunities for small businesses.[11] More importantly, contractors must make a good faith effort to implement the plan or suffer significant penalties. The law is implemented through the clauses at FAR 52.219-9 (Small Business Subcontracting Plan) and FAR 52.219-16 (Liquidated Damages—Subcontracting Plan). FAR 52.219-9(d) essentially provides that:

The [contractor's] subcontracting plan must include:

1. Goals, expressed in terms of percentages of total planned subcontracting dollars, for each category of small business.

2. A statement of

   i. Total dollars planned to be subcontracted for an individual contract plan; or the offeror's total projected sales, expressed in dollars, and the total value of projected subcontracts to support the sales for a commercial plan;

ii. Total dollars planned to be subcontracted to small business concerns;

iii. Total dollars planned to be subcontracted to veteran-owned small business concerns;

iv. Total dollars planned to be subcontracted to service-disabled veteran-owned small business;

v. Total dollars planned to be subcontracted to HUBZone small business concerns;

vi. Total dollars planned to be subcontracted to small disadvantaged business concerns; and

vii. Total dollars planned to be subcontracted to women-owned small business concerns.

3. A description of the principal types of supplies and services to be subcontracted, and an identification of the types planned for subcontracting to—

i. Small business concerns;

ii. Veteran-owned small business concerns;

iii. Service-disabled veteran-owned small business concerns;

iv. HUBZone small business concerns;

v. Small disadvantaged business concerns; and

vi. Women-owned small business concerns.

4. A description of the method used to develop the subcontracting goals.

The clause requires various reports and states that "failure of the [c]ontractor or subcontractor to comply in good faith with…an approved plan required by this clause shall be a material breach of the contract."[12]

The most significant part of this regulatory framework is the potential damages that may be levied upon the contractor if it fails to carry out the plan in good faith. FAR 52.219-16 states that "failure to make a good faith effort to comply with the subcontracting plan…means a willful or intentional failure to perform in accordance with the requirements of the [plan]…or willful or intentional action to frustrate the plan. Performance shall be measured by applying the percentage goals to the total actual subcontracting dollars." FAR 52.219 goes on to say that if the contractor fails to meet its subcontracting goals and "the [c]ontracting [o]fficer decides…that the [c]ontractor failed to make a good faith effort to comply with its subcontracting plan…the [c]ontractor shall pay the [g]overnment liquidated damages…in an amount equal to the actual dollar amount by which the [c]ontractor failed to achieve each subcontract goal."[13]

Where required, contractors must establish a viable subcontracting plan and must make a good faith effort to execute that plan. Failure to do so can result in stiff penalties.

35

You failed to include a specially tailored disputes clause in your subcontract, including a statement that the subcontractor must continue to perform as directed by the prime contractor during the pendency of any dispute.

It is crucial that you include a tailored disputes clause in your subcontracts and that you do not simply flow down the government's disputes clause verbatim, which is not appropriately worded for disputes between private contractors.[14] Here is what the disputes clause in a prime contract states:

This contract is subject to the Contract Disputes Act of 1978, as amended…A claim by the [c]ontractor shall be made in writing and [shall be] submitted… to the [c]ontracting [o]fficer for a written decision… [T]he [c]ontracting [o]fficer must…decide the claim.…The [c]ontracting [o]fficer's decision shall be final unless the [c]ontractor appeals or files a suit as provided in the [Contract Disputes] Act.…The [c]ontractor shall proceed diligently with performance of this contract, pending final resolution of any request for relief, claim, appeal, or action arising under the contract, and comply with any decision of the [c]ontracting [o]fficer.[15]

As you can see, the previous clause cannot be modified easily to serve as a vehicle for disputes between two private parties. For this reason, your subcontracts should contain a tailored disputes clause that includes: (1) a procedure for resolving disputes between the parties; (2) a requirement that, pending resolution of the dispute, the subcontractor must proceed as directed by the prime contractor; and (3) a forum for appeal.

The informal method for resolving disputes in a subcontract may be similar to what is specified in the prime contract's dispute clause; that is, it may provide for a written claim to be submitted to an identified official of the prime contractor for a decision within a stated time period. The subcontract should also indicate a specific forum and manner for appeal of the prime contractor's initial decision (e.g., a state or federal court of appropriate jurisdiction or an alternative dispute resolution forum, such as the American Arbitration Association).

By using a tailored disputes clause, the prime contractor ensures that the subcontractor will continue performing required work and that there will be a reasonable means for settling disputes that protects both the prime and the subcontractor.

ENDNOTES

1. FAR 52.215-2.

2. FAR 52.230-2.

3. FAR 52.222-26.

4. FAR 52.222-6.

5. FAR 52.222-41.

6. FAR 52.243-1 (which states, in part, "the [c]ontracting [o]fficer may at any time…make changes within the general scope of this contract in any one or more of the following: drawings, designs, or specifications…method of shipment…or place of delivery").

7. FAR 52.249-2 (which states, in part, "the [g]overnment may terminate performance of work under this contract in whole or, from time to time, in part if the [c]ontracting [o]fficer determines that a termination is in the [g]overnment's interest").

8. U.C.C. § 2-209.

9. FAR 52.249-8.

10. 15 U.S.C. § 637(d).

11. FAR 19.702.

12. FAR 52.219-9.

13. FAR 52.219-16.

14. FAR 52.233-1.

15. Id.

Chapter 8

Contract Administration

36

You accepted direction from an unauthorized official regarding your obligations under a contract.

Government contract cases are filled with examples of contractors who took direction from officials who had no authority to direct them. The *FAR* states:

> Contracting officers have authority to enter into, administer, or terminate contracts and make related determinations and findings. [They] may bind the [g]overnment only to the extent of the authority delegated to them, [and they] shall receive from the appointing authority clear instructions in writing regarding the limits of their authority. Information on the limits of the contracting officers' authority shall be readily available to the public and agency personnel.[1]

Although not clearly stated in the *FAR*, government personnel and contractors often speak of the officials who possess this authority as "warranted contracting officers."[2]

Contract specialists (who work for contracting officers, or COs) do not possess this inherent authority, nor does a contracting officer's representative (COR); a contracting officer's technical representative (COTR); or any other inspector, auditor, or similar person working for the CO. As a default, only the CO can give you direction, interpret specifications, demand changes, or revise your written contract in any way.

An administrative contracting officer (ACO) refers to a CO who is administering contracts.[3] Contractors frequently confuse the CO, who has contracting authority, with the ACO, who normally does not. The most common CO/ACO split occurs in the Department of Defense (DOD),

where procuring commands employ the CO, but where the contract is administered by the Defense Contract Management Agency (DCMA) and a group of ACOs. Although a CO may delegate his or her authority to an ACO, such delegation is rare.

It is easy to find out if ACOs, CORs, COTRs, or inspectors who seek to direct you or make a change in your contract have the authority to do so—just ask them for their written delegation of authority![4] If it isn't in writing from a CO (or a delegatee), it isn't valid direction under the *FAR*. If they are reluctant to give you copies of their delegation, you should conclude that they possess no such authority and should contact your CO. The case law is filled with contractors who took direction from someone without authority, and the result is almost always the same: the court or board finds against the contractor or denies the claim because the contractor did not comply with the written contract.[5]

Here's an example: In a contract to design, fabricate, install, and maintain exhibits for the United States Pavilion at the 1984 Louisiana World Exhibition in New Orleans, the contractor asserted that it had been directed to perform additional work outside the scope of the contract on theaters and acoustical ceilings. However, the direction had been given by the contract specialist and the COTR. The contract clearly indicated that only the CO had the authority to make changes in the requirements of the contract. Accordingly, the court denied the contractor's claim of constructive change because the directing officials lacked the authority to make such a change. However, where the CO ordered a change involving the installation of drywall, the court found that a constructive change had occurred and that the contractor was entitled to an equitable adjustment.[6]

Similarly, a solicitation's contracting officer is the only person to whom you should direct your questions about the solicitation. While you may communicate with a contracts specialist, a COTR, or a COR, these individuals have no authority to advise you about the solicitation or to issue an amendment to the solicitation.

37

You failed to read your entire contract, including all of the amendments and clauses incorporated by reference.

The written contract is the key to a contractor's obligations and responsibilities. But how many contractors actually read the entire contract before beginning performance? Most read the statement of work (SOW) and proceed from there. But there are other equally critical sections in the uniform contract format[7]—such as Section E, Inspection and Acceptance; Section F, Deliveries or Performance; Section G, Contract Administration Data; and Section H, Special Contract Requirements—that may be equally important.

Indeed, many vital clauses are not even printed in your contract. Almost every government contract includes a clause that permits the government to incorporate clauses by reference.[8] Essentially, the government lists the *FAR* clauses and states, "This contract incorporates one or more clauses by reference, with the same force and effect as if they were given in full text." You can easily obtain the full text on the Internet, or you can ask your CO for a copy. It doesn't matter whether the clauses are printed in your contract in full text or incorporated by reference; you are still responsible for all the duties and obligations contained in them. Indeed, the typical government contract, which might be only 30 pages long, expands to two or three times that length once the clauses incorporated by reference are printed out. Smart contractors print out a copy of all clauses incorporated by reference and insert them into the master contract file before

the contract starts. An experienced government contractor may be able to skip a full reading of particular clauses that are familiar, but there really is no substitute for a detailed, in-depth reading of a contract before performance starts.

Contractors should also be aware that sometimes a clause that is not incorporated into a contract may be read into the contract later by the courts or boards of contract appeal. Where there is a missing mandatory contract clause that expresses a significant or deeply ingrained strand of public procurement policy, it is considered to be included in the contract by operation of law.[9] The termination for convenience clause is such a clause.[10] As you can see, on some occasions, reading the entire contract will still not advise you of all your duties and responsibilities.

With certain minor exceptions that are not worth discussing here, the general rule is that the *FAR* clause in effect at the time of execution of the contract (and presumably included in your solicitation and contract) applies to that contract. It really does not matter if the *FAR* clause is changed and updated one or more times during the performance of your contract. The clause in your contract at the time of award governs your rights and obligations. The government may not change those clauses without your agreement or without permitting you an equitable adjustment resulting from the change.

38

You followed oral promises and direction instead of what was in the written contract.

In government contracts, only the written word is binding. Contractors should learn to politely ignore any oral advice from any government officials, no matter how convincing. The written contract always defines your duties and responsibilities. Reliance on oral advice from unauthorized government employees is at the contractor's risk, and the government is not bound by such advice.[11] This conclusion is particularly true when a government official attempts to make a side deal (e.g., "instead of fixing the faucets in Building 520, as required by the contract, just fix the toilet in the commander's house. We'll call it a wash.") Such oral requests are usually made by government officials who are in pursuit of their own agendas and who do not have legal authority to change the contract. In those circumstances, you must respond diplomatically but otherwise ignore such requests.

The Federal Circuit has dealt with the issue of oral modification to contracts, and the holdings generally do not favor contractors. In *Mil-Spec Contractors, Inc., v. United States*,[12] the court held that "where the pertinent regulations required that contract modifications be written, an oral modification that had not been reduced to writing and signed by both parties was ineffective."[13]

A contract modification means any written change in the terms of a contract,[14] and a change order is a written order directing a contract change by a CO.[15] The answer to the problem of oral modifications is simple: there are no oral modifications. Follow the written contract until you receive an appropriate written change order or supplemental agreement.[16]

39

You failed to comply with the quality control/quality assurance requirements in your contract.

Quality assurance is a crucial aspect of any contract. Contract quality requirements are the "technical requirements in the contract relating to the quality of the product or service and the

clauses prescribing inspection and other quality controls incumbent on the contractor to [ensure] that the end product or service conforms to the contract requirements."[17] FAR 46.202, et seq., lays out four general categories of quality requirements:

1. The standard inspection requirements require the contractor to maintain an acceptable inspection system and to give the government the right to make inspections and test while work is in progress.

2. For the procurement of complex or critical items (higher-level contracts, such as for high-performance aircraft, submarines, etc.), there can be increased quality standards.

3. For commercial items, the government should rely on the contractor's existing quality assurance systems as a substitute for government inspection.

4. For contracts under $100,000, the government may rely on inspections conducted by the contractor.

The government is entitled to insist on strict compliance with the contract's specifications and may order the correction of nonconforming work.[18] Thus, not only must a contractor develop a quality assurance program that complies with the contract's requirements, but the system also has to work. The system must reject nonconforming items and tender only those goods or services that meet the contract. If such a system proves elusive, see a consultant. The consultant's cost will pale in comparison to the cost of swallowing the rejected nonconforming goods.

40

You failed to deliver on time as required by the delivery schedule.

Failure to meet the delivery schedule is a common reason for the government to terminate your contract for default immediately. The fixed-price default clause[19] states that the government may terminate a contract in whole or in part if the contractor fails to deliver the supplies or to perform the services within the time specified in this contract. No cure notice is required.

In cases where the contractor is endangering the contract's timely performance, a cure notice is provided. If the contractor fails to make progress or cure the offending condition within 10 days, the government may terminate the contract for default without waiting for the delivery date to expire. Default is precluded only where the cause for tardiness was beyond the contractor's control and was not caused by the contractor's negligence.[20]

The consequences of a default termination are severe, and the courts call it a "drastic sanction."[21] Not only does a default result in the loss of your current contract, but it also carries two additional consequences. First, the government may acquire supplies or services similar to those terminated, and the contractor will be liable to the government for any excess procurement costs (i.e., the government's cost to procure the goods or services from another source in excess of the price in the terminated contract). This cost could be substantial and could easily bankrupt a small business. Second, the default may result in the loss of future contracts. All government contracts of more than $100,000 are required to include certifications by the contractors stating whether or not they have "within a three-year period preceding [the contract] had one or more contracts terminated for default by any federal agency."[22] COs will likely think twice about awarding you additional contracts with a recent default on your record.

41

You failed to submit a proper invoice.

Cash flow is the lifeblood of every business. Contractors who fail to invoice properly are likely to find themselves short a few quarts, because the government will pay only proper invoices. Therefore, contractors need to understand what the government's payment procedures are and what constitutes a proper invoice.

The Prompt Payment Act[23] (PPA) requires that the government generally make payment on a proper invoice within 30 days of its submission or pay interest penalties on the unpaid amount. The PPA further requires that the agency return any defective invoice (i.e., one that is not proper) within seven days of receipt, with a statement identifying the defect.[24] In practice, returns of defective invoices are relatively rare. Therefore, it is essential that a contractor submit a proper invoice the first time and every time it submits an invoice.

Most fixed-price contracts contain the prompt payment clause,[25] which defines a proper invoice as one that contains the following items:

i.   Name and address of the [c]ontractor.

ii. Invoice date and invoice number.

iii. Contract number or other authorization for supplies delivered or services performed (including order number and contract line item number).

iv. Description, quantity, unit of measure, unit price, and extended price of supplies delivered or services performed.

v.   Shipping and payment terms.

vi. Name and address of [c]ontractor official to whom payment is to be sent (must be the same as that in the contract or in a proper notice of assignment).

vii. Name (where practicable), title, phone number, and mailing address of person to notify in the event of a defective invoice.

viii. Taxpayer Identification Number (TIN).

ix. Electronic funds transfer (EFT) banking information.

x. Any other information or documentation required by the contract (e.g., evidence of shipment).

The PPA regulations[26] require the same elements. In addition, the contract may include other special requirements for the submission of invoices. The omission of any one element renders the invoice defective (e.g., the simple omission of a contract line item number on the invoice).

Contractors who submit an initial improper invoice in a contract requiring recurring invoices (such as for services or leases) run the risk of the government repeatedly failing to pay their invoices—particularly where invoicing is automated. Frequently there will be little to no notice of the government's rejection of invoices. The contractor simply sees its invoices go unpaid.

The solution to the problem is simple. Consult your contract and FAR 52.232-25 (and any other payment clauses in your contract) before preparing the first invoice. Ensure that the first invoice is proper, and instruct your personnel that all subsequent invoices must follow the outline of the first. Finally, if an invoice is not paid within 45 days of its submission, follow up immediately with the CO to determine where the problem lies. If re-invoicing is necessary, so be it. At least you will have learned how to submit a proper invoice for all subsequent billings under the contract.

42

You failed to follow up on nonpayment of proper invoices.

Surprisingly, many contractors are somewhat cavalier about seeking monies owed to them under their government contracts. In addition, they often fail to follow up on the nonpayment of properly submitted invoices, despite the PPA, which requires a proper invoice's payment within 30 days.[27]

The longer a contractor waits, either to submit a proper invoice for monies owed or to follow up on a properly submitted invoice, the more difficult it becomes to resolve the problem later. As time passes, memories fade, records are lost, and personnel transfer.

A true but anonymous story: A small business submitted invoices a full five months after the money was owed under its contract. When the contractor finally submitted the invoices, the agency was confused as to the amounts owed and for what periods, leading the agency to spend another several months reviewing the invoices. Finally, the contractor wrote to the CO, who issued a formal decision stating that the agency owed the company more than $250,000. Unfortunately, another 30 days passed with the agency's finance office failing to pay the invoices, despite the CO's decision. Almost eight months after the work was completed, the company finally came to counsel, seeking help in collecting the funds owed. Although the counsel was happy to accept a new client and successfully recovered the amount owed, the whole affair probably could have been avoided if the contractor had simply invoiced the agency in a timely fashion.

As a government contractor, you should develop a system that ensures that every invoice is proper, that it fully complies with all contractual requirements, that it is sent to the address stated in the contract, and that it is submitted shortly after money is owed. If you do not receive payment within 45 days, write to the CO and insist that the invoice be paid within seven days (or if it was not a proper invoice, correct and resubmit it). Finally, if you are not paid within seven days, obtain counsel and submit a claim for nonpayment of a proper invoice.

43

You volunteered to perform extra work with the expectation that you would be compensated later.

Volunteers embark on duties of their own free will and without any expectation that they will be paid for the work. Government contractors frequently fall into this category in a desire to please their clients. If a contractor freely elects to perform work not required by a contract without a formal change order, the contractor is considered to be a volunteer who will not be paid for the services.[28] Contractors should be wary of any situation where the government asks for services or performance not included in the contract. To be compensated for such a constructive change, the contractor must identify the work, notify the CO, and request an appropriate change order and equitable adjustment.

44

When your labor costs increased as the result of a new wage determination or collective bargaining agreement, or as the result of continued compliance with a pre-existing wage determination or collective bargaining agreement, you failed to claim a price adjustment pursuant to the Service Contract Act.

The Fair Labor Standards Act and Service Contract Act Price Adjustment Clause for Multiple Year and Option Contracts[29] (the price adjustment clause) provides that a government contract's price will be adjusted to reflect a contractor's actual increase or decrease in applicable wages and fringe benefits where the contract is subject to prevailing wage determinations and collective bargaining agreements (i.e., it protects contractors from mandated increases in labor costs as a result of Department of Labor wage determinations or collective bargaining agreements [CBAs]).

The U.S. Court of Appeals for the Federal Circuit recently held that a contractor may receive a price increase under this clause—even when there is no change in the mandated benefit—if there is a change in the cost of providing that benefit. In *Lear Siegler Servs., Inc., v. Rumsfeld*,[30] the Air Force awarded Lear Siegler Services, Inc. (LSI), a contract for aircraft maintenance. The contract incorporated the terms of the Service Contract Act (SCA), including the price adjustment clause. LSI's CBA required it to provide its employees with a defined-benefit health plan; a plan that obligated LSI to spend whatever was necessary to continue to provide its employees with an agreed-upon level of benefit, even as the costs of providing that benefit rose. LSI submitted a claim for the increased costs of maintaining the defined-benefit health plan, pursuant to the price adjustment clause. The Air Force denied the request. On appeal, the Armed Services Board of Contract Appeals (ASBCA) held that there had been no change in the terms of the CBA; hence, the price adjustment clause did not apply.

The Federal Circuit reversed the decision, explaining that a wage determination or CBA that requires future increases in fringe benefits triggers the government's obligations under the price adjustment clause. The court concluded that "the [p]rice [a]djustment clause is triggered by changes in an employer's cost of compliance with the terms of a wage determination. The fact that there has been no nominal change in the mandated benefit (i.e., that there has been no change in the level of benefit provided by the defined-benefit plan) is simply irrelevant."

Most service contractors understand that when they have contracts subject to the SCA, they should submit claims for price adjustments subsequent to new wage determinations or CBAs. However, as *Lear* illustrates, a service contractor is also entitled to a price adjustment where there is an increased cost in continued compliance with pre-existing wage determinations or CBAs.

45

You failed to realize that you have no right to receive an option.

Although government contracts often include a variety of priced options for increased quantities or extensions of the performance period, those options are unilateral and are available at the government's discretion and judgment. The contractor does not have a right to receive such options. Never assume that the government will automatically exercise any of the options in your contract.

FAR Subpart 17.2 governs the award and exercise of options. It specifically states that a CO may exercise an option only if the following exist:

- Funds are available;

- There is a government need;

- The option is the most advantageous method of fulfilling the government's need, when price and other factors are considered; and

- The option was synopsized, if required.

Case law clearly relates that the government's failure to exercise an option in a contract does not ordinarily give rise to a breach of contract action. A standard option provision in a government contract obliges the contractor to perform the additional contract work if the government chooses to exercise the option, but it does not create a legal obligation on the part of the government to exercise the option and require the work.[31] Therefore, counting on the government's exercise of priced options in your contract is a little like counting your chickens before they're hatched.

46

You failed to realize that the government has a unilateral right to extend a contract for services for up to six months.

Whether performing a one-year services contract or the last year in the fourth option year of a services contract, do not assume that when the contract performance period ends, your obligation ends with it. While not mandatory, virtually all contracts for services (guard services, engineering services, mechanical services, trash removal services, information technology services, etc.) include the option to extend services clause,[32] which states, as follows:

The [g]overnment may require continued performance of any services within the limits and at the rates specified in the contract. These rates may be adjusted only as a result of revisions to prevailing labor rates provided by the Secretary of Labor. The option provision may be exercised more than once, but the total extension of performance hereunder shall not exceed 6 months. The [c]ontracting [o]fficer may exercise the option by written notice to the [c]ontractor within ___ [insert the period of time within which the (c)ontracting (o)fficer may exercise the option].

The clause gives agencies flexibility in replacing an outgoing contractor and is frequently used to extend performance when there is a bid protest at the Government Accountability Office (GAO) or the Court of Federal Claims, so there is no break in needed services. As noted in the clause, this right may be exercised multiple times (e.g., once per month), but the total extension of performance may not exceed six months.

47

You continued to work on a multi-year contract after the end of the current year on the promise that the option year would be exercised, even though it had not been formally exercised by the government.

In a multi-year contract, a major disruption is likely to occur when a contractor ceases work at the end of any given year because funds (and thus a signed contract or option) for the next year have not been made available. This work stoppage inevitably leads government officials to ask the contractor to continue work on the promise that the option year will be exercised as soon as funds are available. Contractors should resist this temptation and—tactfully—demand that the CO exercise the

option and provide the necessary funding. Absent the formal exercise of the option, there is no legal obligation of the government to pay the contractor for the work.

Contracts with several option years typically contain a clause that specifies the availability of funds for the next fiscal year[33] and that states the following:

Funds are not presently available for performance under this contract beyond ___. The [g]overnment's obligation for performance of this contract beyond that date is contingent upon the availability of appropriated funds from which payment for contract purposes can be made. No legal liability on the part of the [g]overnment for any payment may arise for performance under this contract beyond ___, until funds are made available to the [c]ontracting [o]fficer for performance and until the [c]ontractor receives notice of availability, to be confirmed in writing by the [c]ontracting [o]fficer.

The clause is included because, under the Anti-Deficiency Act,[34] the CO may not lawfully commit the government beyond the agency's presently available appropriation, which normally is available for a single year only.

The fact that new funds are not yet available does not mean that a CO is without resources. Sometimes COs have funds that can be diverted or recaptured from another purpose and can be obligated to the continuation of a multi-year contract.

A contractor should generally advise its CO that without a valid contract, it will efficiently close down the contract operation at the end of the contract performance period. If COs want to avoid the disruption that will occur, they need to exercise the option (with funds) or award an entirely separately funded contract altogether.

48

You failed to demand that the government exercise any option in strict accord with the terms of that option.

A contractor should insist that the government exercise its unilateral options in strict accord with the terms of the contract. In a government contract, an option is basically a contract to keep a contractor's offer open for a prescribed period, during which period the offer is irrevocable.[35] The option binds the government to do nothing, but grants the government the right to accept or reject the offer in accordance with its terms within the time period and in the manner specified in the option.[36] The exercise of an option is effective only when received by the contractor.[37] The exercise of an out-of-time option is ineffective;[38] however, performance of the option period under protest entitles the contractor to an equitable adjustment pursuant to the changes clause.[39]

Typically, government contracts with options include language requiring the government to provide notice of its intent to exercise the option 60 days in advance. Even the preliminary notice of intent to exercise must be received on time or the option exercise is ineffective.[40] The preliminary notice is an integral component of the process by which the government binds the contractor to another contract term, and it must be performed by the government in a timely and correct manner.

In the exercise of an option, any attempt by the government to alter the conditions of the contractor's obligation, such as the period of performance, will render ineffective the purported exercise of an option. Moreover, insertion of an availability of funds clause, limiting the government's liability for payment, renders the option exercise conditional and invalid.[41]

If options are not exercised in strict accord with the contract, the contractor has two possible choices. Either the contractor may reject the option outright, or the contractor may choose to accept the option and demand an equitable adjustment in price. In fixed price contracts, it is frequently the case that by the time the option comes around, the fixed pricing included therein is less profitable for the contractor as a result of increased costs. A misstep by the government in the exercise of the option can provide a contractor with the needed opportunity to remove itself from an otherwise burdensome contract.

49

On the promise of award, you started to work and incurred costs before your contract was actually signed.

In government contracting, there can be numerous snags before a contract is actually signed. There may be additional review levels above the CO who actually signs the contract, or there may simply be funding issues that make it impossible for a CO to sign a contract. Regardless of the issues involved, no contractor should initiate performance or incur costs until it receives a signed copy of the contract award. Starting work prior to formal award of a contract results in significant risk of nonpayment to the contractor.

A contractor may receive a written letter outlining the government's intent to award the contract, but that letter is not a contract award. Only an actual award of a contract on the requisite government form or a letter contract constitutes an award. The government frequently awards unfunded contracts, which contain a clause stating that the government has no legal liability for any payment until funds are available, and the contractor is so notified in writing.[42] An unfunded contract is, simply stated, not a contract at all because there is no consideration. A contractor should never succumb to government requests to begin work without a signed contract. Contractor costs and liability are far too great; without a signed contract, the government's liabilities are generally zero.

The lack of a signed contract can pose extreme problems when the contractor is the incumbent for a follow-on contract, either in the form of a new contract or the exercise of an option. There is a very serious question surrounding whether the contractor should suspend work while waiting for a new contract, the signed exercise of an option, or new funding. Would such a suspension be disruptive to the government and the contractor's workforce? The answer to both questions is, of course, *yes*, but that should not sway the contractor. Even if suspension of performance would be disruptive, the contractor should never place itself in the position of providing goods and services to the government when no mutuality of obligation exists between the parties. This is just plain good business sense.

By the same token, no contractor should begin work if its contract or any government correspondence states that funding for the contract is "not presently available." Until the contractor receives written confirmation that funds are available for its particular contract, the contractor is unlikely to be paid for any work.

50

You failed to pay the minimum wages or benefits required by the wage determination in your contract.

Failure to pay the minimum wages and benefits required by a wage determination in a contract subject to either the Davis-Bacon Act or the SCA

of 1965 may result in severe sanctions including financial penalties, debarment, and criminal prosecution.

Federal construction contracts for more than $2,000, and federal contracts for the provision of services worth more than $2,500, are required to include minimum wages and fringe benefits. Contractors should receive a wage determination in the solicitation and contract identifying minimum wages and benefits for all categories of employees. Those minimum wages have been established to ensure that federal contractors are paid prevailing wages. Construction contracts include the Davis-Bacon Act clause,[43] while federal service contracts include the SCA clause.[44]

It is important to note that the minimum wages and benefits apply to not only the prime contract, but also all subcontracts. In construction contracts, the clause states that "[a]ll laborers and mechanics employed or working upon the site of the work will be paid [minimum amounts specified in the contract]."[45] In service contracts, the clause requires prime contractors to pay the minimum wages, and it states that the "contractor agrees to insert this clause in all subcontracts subject to the [a]ct."[46] The prime contractor is responsible for any underpayments made by its subcontractors.[47] Of course, the prime contractor will attempt to extract the underpayments from the errant subcontractor, but this may prove impossible if the subcontractor is insolvent or is in the midst of bankruptcy proceedings.

Labor audits performed by the Department of Labor Wage and Hours Division will identify those contractors who fail to provide the requisite minimum wages and fringe benefits. The resulting consequences can be quite severe and can include the following:

- Withholding of funds owed to the contractor and use of those funds to pay the unpaid wages or benefits;[48]

- Debarment of the contractor (i.e., preventing it from receiving any future federal contracts for a period of up to three years);[49]

- Referral to the attorney general for prosecution, where there are willful or aggravated violations;[50] or

- Cancellation of the contract.[51]

51

You requested a revision to the delivery schedule for reasons other than government delay or fault, but you failed to offer consideration (generally a price reduction).

Article 2 of the Uniform Commercial Code, adopted by 49 of the 50 states,[52] indicates that an agreement modifying a contract needs no consideration to be binding.[53] However, that is not the case in government contracts. In government contracts, a contract may not be modified without consideration.[54] The *FAR* states that "if the contractor fails to perform an order, or [to] take appropriate corrective action, the ordering activity may terminate the order for cause or modify the order to establish a new delivery date (after obtaining consideration, as appropriate)."[55]

Because a change in the delivery schedule is a modification to the contract, COs are unable to accept a contractor's proposed change without obtaining some form of consideration, be it monetary or otherwise (e.g., an increase in the warranty provisions, accelerated delivery, etc.). If a contractor fails to offer consideration, typically the CO will reject the requested modification to the delivery schedule, and the contractor will run the risk of default. A good example of this principal can be found in *Automated Power Sys.,*

Inc.,[56] where "[t]he contracting officer stated that without consideration the requested extension would not have been granted and appellant would have been in default of the contract. The $200, therefore, constituted the necessary consideration for extending the contract performance date."

52

You failed to appreciate the extent of the government's rights in data or software.

Most contractors fail to read solicitations or contracts carefully, as noted previously in this book. The rights in data and software clauses are no exception and constitute an area where many contractors pay a steep price for their complacency. Through those clauses, the government will typically grant itself rights in your contract that permit the government to supply your data or software to your competitors, unless you take appropriate action.

The two most frequently used clauses are the rights in technical data: the noncommercial items clause[57] and the rights in noncommercial computer software and noncommercial computer software documentation clause.[58] In both, the government will obtain one of three types of rights in what you might otherwise consider to be your proprietary data or software:

1. **Unlimited rights**—The government has unlimited rights in technical data and computer software developed exclusively with government funds and in computer software documentation required to be delivered under the contract.

2. **Government purpose rights**—The government has government purpose rights for a five-year period, or such other period as may

be negotiated for technical data or computer software that was developed with mixed funding (i.e., development was accomplished with costs charged to indirect cost pools or costs not allocated to a government contract, and partially with costs charged directly to a government contract). The government may not use data or software for which it has government purpose rights for commercial purposes, but it may release or disclose the data outside the government for government purposes, such as the development of a second source or a competition designed to reduce the price of an item.[59]

3. **Limited rights**—The government obtains limited rights in items, components, processes, or software developed exclusively at private expense and marked with an appropriate legend. Limited rights mean the right to use, modify, reproduce, release, perform, display, or disclose technical data, in whole or in part, within the government.[60] The government and the contractor may negotiate for additional limited rights.

It is important to note that the *Defense Federal Acquisition Regulation Supplement* (*DFARS*) indicates the following:

> In unusual situations, the standard rights may not satisfy the [g]overnment's needs, or the [g]overnment may be willing to accept lesser rights in data or in computer software in return for other consideration. In those cases, a special license may be negotiated. However, the licensor is not obligated to provide the [g]overnment greater rights and the contracting officer is not required to accept lesser rights than the rights provided in the standard grant of license.[61]

This statement means that a contractor may negotiate during the formation of a contract for the preservation of rights that otherwise would transfer to the government. For example, a contractor

could offer consideration (typically a reduction in price) to reduce the government's otherwise unlimited rights to government-purpose rights or limited rights. Where you feel the disclosure of this information will result in a loss of competitive position, it may well be worth a try to conduct such a negotiation.

53

You failed to assert your right to an equitable adjustment in a timely manner.

The changes clause[62] requires that the contractor "assert its right to an adjustment [when there is a change] within 30 days from the date of receipt of the written [change] order [or the constructive change]." Thus, it would seem that a failure to assert your right to an equitable adjustment in writing in a timely fashion would result in the outright denial of your equitable adjustment or claim. Although this possibility exists, the courts and boards have been unwilling to accept such a harsh result under certain circumstances and have indicated, for example, in *Hoel-Steffen Construction Company v. United States*,[63] that written notice requirements should not be construed hyper-technically to deny legitimate contractor claims when the government is "otherwise aware of the operative facts."[64] Where responsible government officials are aware or should be aware of the facts giving rise to a claim, strict compliance with a contract's written notice requirements is not required.[65] Even oral notice may be furnished to responsible government representatives.[66] The burden is on the government to establish that it was prejudiced by the absence of the required notice.

In *Kumin Associates, Inc.*,[67] the government argued that the contractor was not entitled to an equitable adjustment for a constructive change because it did not provide written notice of the constructive change to the CO in accordance with the notification of changes clause. The board rejected this argument, stating that contractor personnel orally notified the government's project manager, an authorized consultant of the CO, of the out-of-scope work, which was sufficient under the circumstances. The board reaffirmed that written notice requirements are construed liberally where the CO has actual or imputed knowledge of the pertinent facts, or where the lack of notice was not prejudicial.

Notwithstanding the boards' and courts' leniency in these matters, contractors are urged to provide their COs with immediate written notice of their intent to seek an equitable adjustment for written or constructive changes in order to preserve their right to a time delay or cost increase. Unlike in the cases cited earlier, the CO may or may not be unaware of the operative facts, and the lack of notice may, indeed, prejudice the government.

54

You failed to realize that you have a duty to continue contract performance, despite a burdensome change order.

Contractors who are unhappy about a change order, or some other explicit direction from a CO, must remember their obligation to continue contract performance pursuant to the Contract Disputes Act and the disputes clause.

The Contract Disputes Act states:

> [A] contracting officer's decision on [a] claim shall be final and conclusive [and nothing shall] prohibit executive agencies from including a clause in government contracts requiring that pending final decision of an appeal, action, or final settlement; *a contractor shall proceed diligently with performance of the contract in accordance with the contracting officer's decision.*[68]

The standard government disputes clause states that "[t]he [c]ontractor shall proceed diligently with performance of this contract, pending final resolution of any request for relief, claim, appeal, or action arising under the contract, and [shall] comply with any decision of the [c]ontracting [o]fficer."[69]

Alliant Techsystems, Inc., v. United States[70] indicates that there is only one circumstance under which an unhappy contractor may refuse to perform while its dispute is pending: where the government commits a material breach of the contract.[71] Thus,

> [T]he government may not, through a contracting officer's decision, impose obligations on a contractor far exceeding any contemplated by [the] contract. If the government orders a "drastic modification" in the performance [or payment terms] required by the contract, the order is considered a "cardinal change" that constitutes a material breach of the contract… Such a material breach has the effect of freeing the contractor of its obligations under the contract, including its obligations under the disputes clause.[72]

Therefore, even if a contractor is not satisfied with a change order or other direction from the CO, unless there is a material breach of contract on the part of the government, the contractor must continue with satisfactory performance, or its contract may be terminated for default.

55

You failed to appreciate the difference between anticipatory repudiation and negotiation.

As previously discussed, when a contractor refuses to perform where the government has not materially breached the contract, the government is within its rights to terminate the contractor for default. The rights of the government when a contractor repudiates performance are similar to what is provided in the Uniform Commercial Code (UCC) at Section 2-610, Anticipatory Repudiation. Under the UCC, the nonrepudiating contractor can await performance or resort to breach (default) remedies. The government essentially enjoys the same rights when a contractor repudiates performance. The term generally used is "anticipatory repudiation," because the contractor is stating in advance that it will not perform, even though it has not formally stopped performing.

The standard for anticipatory repudiation is when one party to a contract absolutely refuses to perform a contract and, before the time arrives for performance, distinctly and unqualifiedly communicates that refusal to the other party; the other party can, if it chooses, treat the refusal as a breach and, therefore, can commence an action at once.[73] For one to be a true anticipatory repudiation, there must be a "positive, definite, unconditional, and unequivocal manifestation of intent—on the part of the contractor—of its intent not to perform."[74] If such positive and definite intent has been given, the CO may terminate the contract forthwith on the grounds of anticipatory breach.

In *Cascade Pacific*,[75] the contractor was required to provide spring hinges to the General Services Administration (GSA). The specifications required the hinges to be plated with a particular finish. Cascade Pacific attempted to provide painted (nonspecification) hinges and requested a change in the specification to painted hinges. GSA refused to accept painted spring hinges in lieu of plated ones. Shortly thereafter, Cascade Pacific informed GSA that if it would not accept painted in lieu of plated spring hinges, "we will be unable to perform." Cascade Pacific then missed its deliveries on 13 of 15 orders, and GSA defaulted the contract.

Contrast *Cascade Pacific* with *David/Randall Assoc., Inc., v. Dept. of the Interior*,[76] where the board found a default termination that was based on anticipatory repudiation to be improper.

Indeed, *David/Randall* is an excellent example of how rigorously the standards will be applied. The National Park Service was not happy with Randall's performance on a roofing contract in the Valley Forge National Historical Park. The Park Service suspended the contract, engaged a consultant, and asked Randall if it intended to perform. After an exchange of letters and e-mails, Randall wrote to the government:

> It is David/Randall's intention, upon satisfactory resolution of a number of outstanding issues, to complete performance of the suspended project. Those outstanding issues which require resolution include, inter alia, proper definition of the scope of remaining work, properly addressing the structural issues—which impede David/Randall Associates' negotiations of reasonable extensions of time as well as reasonable schedule for completion, and reimbursement of costs incurred by David/Randall as a result of the suspension (labor and material escalation, home office overhead, remobilization costs, etc.).

The CO terminated the contract for default based solely on the quoted communication. But was this default termination based on a true anticipatory repudiation by the contractor? The board said that it was very clear that it was not. The board said that Randall never absolutely refused to perform. Rather, the company stated it would perform upon the resolution of certain issues.

> Randall was not issuing ultimatums; it was attempting to work with the Park Service to resolve problems. In the e-mail message Randall was stating its willingness to perform and at the same time trying to get to a situation where it could reasonably begin performance after a considerable suspension period. The statements contained in the e-mail were not clearly unreasonable.

These cases clearly demonstrate that if a contractor intends to repudiate a contract and not perform, it must provide a positive, definite, unconditional, and unequivocal communication to that effect. An example would be a letter to the CO stating, "After May 5, Contractor, Inc., will no longer perform in accordance with this contract." However, if you are simply trying to informally resolve a dispute, you should make reasonable demands, as Randall did in the earlier example. Avoid unequivocal statements that you have decided to abandon performance.

56

You failed to comply with the limitation of cost or limitation of funds clause in your contract.

Failure to monitor a cost-reimbursement contract, or to report costs incurred to the CO as required, could mean that the government will not be obligated to pay the contractor above the estimated amounts set forth in the contract. This failure could result in significant losses for a contractor.

In cost-reimbursement contracts, the government is particularly interested in controlling the contractor's actual spending. This control is accomplished by use of either the limitation of cost (LOC) clause,[77] if the contract is fully funded at the outset, or the limitation of funds (LOF) clause,[78] if the contract is incrementally funded. A cost-reimbursement contract must contain one clause or the other.[79]

For both types of contracts, the government must set forth the estimated cost of performance in the contract. The government is not required to reimburse the contractor for any costs above the estimated costs, unless the contractor provides the CO with notice of any expected cost overrun.[80] The contractor can recover the anticipated overrun, subject to the following conditions:

(1) [T]he contractor [must] notify the contracting officer in writing when it anticipates that within the next sixty days it will exceed seventy-five percent of

the estimated cost and provide a revised estimate; (2) [T]he contractor must notify the contracting officer that the total cost of the contract will be significantly greater than estimated; (3) [T]he contracting officer [must] notify the contractor in writing that the estimated cost has been increased by a specific amount; and (4) [U]ntil the contracting officer gives such notice, the contractor is not required to continue performance or incur costs that exceed those estimated in the contract.[81]

In the event the contractor does not receive the government's advance approval, the contractor has the right to refuse work that will cause it to exceed the estimated costs.[82] However, if the contractor does not notify the CO as stated earlier, the government is not obligated to reimburse the contractor for any overrun.[83] After receiving notice of the anticipated overrun, the CO has discretion to approve funding for the overrun, to modify the contractor's work so as to prevent the overrun, or to terminate the contract.[84] And, of course, the contractor must comply with the CO's written decision in order to obtain a full reimbursement later.

In *Titan Corp. v. West*,[85] the contract was a cost plus fixed fee contract that contained the LOC clause. During the period of contract performance, a subsidiary of the Titan Corp. incurred an increase in overhead and administrative costs, triggering the reporting requirements of the LOC clause. Titan's accounting records reflected those costs. The court held that Titan knew, or should have known, that its indirect costs, as they were incurred, exceeded the rates in the contract. Titan pointed to the pressures of work as the reason why it did not notify the government of the anticipated overrun. The court rejected this excuse and noted that the contractor has a duty to monitor its costs and an obligation to inform the government of probable overruns before they occur. The court noted that there was:

…sound reason for the notice requirement of the [l]imitation of [c]osts provision. It protects the contractor by either providing assurance of reimbursement or permitting the contractor to cease performance. It protects the government from paying more than it had expected for the project. The choice as to whether to incur additional costs is the government's not the contractor's.[86]

In summary, the court held that the government was not liable for costs in excess of those estimated in the contract because of Titan's failure to notify the government of the potential overrun.

57

You improperly reported on the source of your components or violated the Buy American Act or Trade Agreements Act in the performance of your contract.

In an attempt to protect American companies and jobs, the Buy American Act (BAA)[87] was enacted to establish a preference for domestic products purchased for public use. The Trade Agreements Act (TAA),[88] conversely, essentially waives the BAA and allows for the purchase of eligible end products from countries that have signed an international trade agreement with the United States or that meet other criteria, such as being a least-developed country.[89] In practice, the combination of the BAA and TAA limit a government contractor's range of foreign sources for both supplies and labor. Although the BAA and TAA are civil laws, violations frequently arise in conjunction with criminal conduct and are, therefore, used to justify increased sentences for convicted persons.

Consequences for breaching the BAA or TAA include debarment, increased penalties under sentencing guidelines, and termination for default.

Debarment—In one case, the Air Force first debarred Glazer Construction for three years, retroactive to February 24, 1998, on the basis of (1) violations of the BAA that were committed during performance of a contract at Hanscom Air Force Base and (2) false statements made to the Air Force during the government's subsequent investigation. Later, the Air Force extended the debarment to an additional six years on the basis of violations of the Davis-Bacon Act and the BAA that were committed by Glazer Construction during performance of a contract in Bedford, Virginia. Finally, the Air Force extended the debarment a second time, again for an additional six years, on the basis of additional BAA violations that were committed by Glazer Construction during its performance on the Bedford, Virginia contract.[90]

Increased Penalties Under Sentencing

Guidelines—In *U.S. v. Electrodyne Systems Corp.*,[91] the court explained how violations of the BAA by individual defendants warranted an upward departure from the U.S. sentencing guidelines. The court stated:

> As mentioned, the Buy American Act was enacted to protect American industry and labor. Instead of complying with the Buy American clauses contained in the [c]ontracts, the [i]ndividual [d]efendants contacted Russian and Ukrainian corporations which could manufacture necessary parts at a discount thereby increasing the profits Electrodyne and Nathan would receive.[92]

[This case was ultimately remanded.]

Termination for Default—In *Sunox, Inc.*,[93] the Defense Logistics Agency terminated Sunox's contract for default because Sunox improperly certified that it complied with the BAA and was providing domestic end products but, in fact, was providing nondomestic end products. The default termination was sustained by the ASBCA.

58

You failed to maintain your present responsibility.

The *FAR* states that purchases shall be made from and contracts awarded only to responsible contractors.[94] To be considered a "responsible contractor," a contractor must:

- Have adequate financial resources to perform the contract, or the ability to obtain them;

- Be able to comply with the required or proposed delivery or performance schedule, taking into consideration all existing commercial and governmental business commitments;

- Have a satisfactory performance record;

- Have a satisfactory record of integrity and business ethics;

- Have the necessary organization, experience, accounting and operational controls, and technical skills, or the ability to obtain them (including, as appropriate, such elements as production control procedures, property control systems, quality assurance measures, and safety programs applicable to materials to be produced or services to be performed by the prospective contractor and subcontractors);

- Have the necessary production, construction, and technical equipment and facilities, or the ability to obtain them; and

- Be otherwise qualified and eligible to receive an award under applicable laws and regulations. [95]

The *FAR* makes it clear (1) that responsibility is an ongoing matter for all contractors and (2) that they must continuously maintain proper organizations, accounting and operational controls, technical skills, production control procedures, property control systems, quality assurance systems, and safety programs as are appropriate to the particular type of contracts they perform. Anything less, and a contractor runs the risk of being found not presently responsible.

59

Your actions resulted in suspension or debarment.

Even more serious than the loss of a present responsibility determination in a particular contract action is a finding of suspension or debarment. During the period of suspension or debarment, a government contractor is ineligible for any future contract awards, may not receive the government's consent to receive a government subcontract, and may not do business with the government as agents or representatives of others.[96] Although debarred or suspended contractors may finish contracts that were in place at the time of the debarment or suspension, the government may not add work, exercise options, or otherwise extend the duration of current contracts or orders.[97]

Debarment can occur for the commission of any offense "indicating a lack of business integrity or business honesty that seriously and directly affects the present responsibility of a [g]overnment contractor or subcontractor."[98] Examples include a civil or criminal finding of fraud, criminal offenses in connection with obtaining or performing a government contract or subcontract, a violation of antitrust statutes, embezzlement, theft, forgery, bribery, falsification or destruction of records, making false statements, tax evasion, or receiving stolen property.

Although debarment is normally effective for three years, similar consequences result if a contractor is suspended. Suspension is an interim measure that may be taken as a result of adequate evidence (including an indictment) showing the commission of acts constituting a basis for debarment as outlined previously.[99]

Although the consequences of a contractor losing its status of present responsibility are serious, the consequences of a suspension or debarment are grave. Small government contractors, in particular, will likely face bankruptcy in the absence of other commercial business. If you are facing suspension or debarment, contact an experienced government contracts attorney immediately.

60

You failed to contest an irrational debarment or suspension.

The *FAR* explains that debarment is a discretionary action, and agency officials have wide latitude to decide whether it is proper in any given case.[100] However, debarment may be imposed "only in the public interest for the [g]overnment's protection and not for purposes of punishment."[101] The *FAR* also states that "[t]he existence of a cause for debarment...does not necessarily require that the contractor be debarred."[102] Before arriving at any debarment decision, the debarment official (DO) is required to consider "the seriousness of the contractor's acts or omissions and any remedial measures or mitigating factors" that are relevant.[103] Although the "existence or nonexistence of any mitigating factors or remedial measures...is not necessarily determinative of a contractor's present responsibility," the DO must consider such factors.

Considering the gravity of debarment and suspension, contractors should challenge—in

district court, if at all possible—any improper debarment action taken by an administrative agency. Unfortunately for contractors, the court will apply a deferential standard of review that allows the court to set aside agency action only if it is "arbitrary, capricious, an abuse of discretion, or otherwise not in accordance with law," or "without observance of procedure required by law."[104] This bar is an extremely low one for the agency to meet—meaning reversal of debarment actions is rare. Yet, it does happen.

In *Canales v. Paulson*,[105] Canales successfully overturned an irrational three-year debarment imposed by the Treasury Department. Between 1999 and 2002, Maria Canales was employed by the U.S. Department of the Treasury. In 2002, she held the title of acting deputy assistant secretary and acting chief information officer. She resigned in October 2002. Before her resignation, on June 1, 2002, Canales incorporated a company, M Squared, which provided management consulting services primarily to government agencies. Canales was the sole shareholder of M Squared and served as its chief executive officer.

In October 2001, while Canales was still employed at the Treasury Department, the department allocated $5.7 million for contracts relating to cyber-security software and consulting services. At that time, John M. Neal, an individual with whom Canales had been acquainted for several years, was working as a consultant for companies seeking those contracts. Although the department was considering various bids, including bids from companies that Neal was representing, Canales and her husband vacationed in Malta with Neal and stayed at a time-share property belonging to Neal's companion. Subsequently, Canales received a Greek vase and several emerald chips from Neal.

In March 2002, the Treasury Department awarded a sole source subcontract worth $1.5 million to one of the companies that Neal represented.

Canales signed the sole source justification for that subcontract. Later, in March 2002, the Treasury's Office of the Inspector General (OIG) began investigating allegations that there was a connection between Canales's relationship with Neal and the award of a sole source subcontract to Neal's client. On June 6, 2002, a representative from the OIG interviewed Canales regarding the gifts she received from Neal. In the course of that interview, Canales made false statements, which were later memorialized in an affidavit she signed, including her denying that she had received emerald chips. Those false statements led Canales to plead guilty to a one-count criminal information[106] in April 2004, charging her with making a false writing during an investigation. The court sentenced Canales to a term of probation. Her plea agreement, and the government's allocution at her sentencing, made clear that no connection had been established between the gifts Canales received and the contract Neal's client won. The government specifically stated in its allocution that there was "no allegation that Canales broke any of the bribery or gratuity laws or corruption offenses" and that her sole offense was making a "false written statement to the [i]nspector [g]eneral."[107]

In November 2005, the Treasury Department initiated proceedings to debar Canales. Canales, through counsel, argued, among other things, that a consideration of several mitigating factors would counsel against debarment. Without accepting the mitigating factors, the debarment official in June 2006 debarred Canales for "conviction of a criminal offense, specifically, making a false writing in connection with an ongoing procurement."[108]

The court found that Canales's debarment was procedurally and substantively invalid. During her debarment proceedings, Canales presented several mitigating factors to the DO. These factors included her spotless record before her criminal offense,

the fact that five years had passed without incident since that offense, and her extensive business with several other federal agencies in the interim—all of which were aware of her misdemeanor conviction when they chose to contract with her. In the debarment notice that he issued to Canales, the DO acknowledged her argument that her "'spotless record' prior to the offense and business record since militate against imposition of debarment" but explained that "I do not agree. Given the facts and nature of your offense, debarment is the appropriate course of action." Nothing in the debarment notice or the administrative record explained the DO's reasoning in coming to this conclusion.

The DO's failure to address in any detail the mitigating factors that Canales raised or to explain why he gave them so little weight made it impossible for the court to evaluate whether there was a rational connection between the facts of her case and the DO's decision to impose debarment. Without such evidence, the court could not conclude that the DO had followed the FAR's requirement that he consider mitigating factors before debarring Canales and thus could not "properly exercise its limited review of the substance of [his] decision."[109]

If you are ever facing an irrational, arbitrary, or capricious debarment, your company (and possibly your personal fortune) may well depend on challenging the debarment in an appropriate U.S. District Court.

61

You failed to recognize that both the contractor and the government have a duty to cooperate in the execution of the contract.

Although the requirement that a contractor cooperate with the government is evident to any government contractor, it is important to remember that cooperation is a two-way street; the government also has a duty to cooperate with the contractor and not to hinder contract performance.

Every contract, as an aspect of the duty of good faith and fair dealing, imposes an implied obligation that neither party will do anything that will hinder or delay the other party in performance of the contract.[110] There is an implied duty to cooperate, which is encompassed within the duty of good faith and fair dealing implied in every government contract.[111] Subterfuges and evasions violate this obligation of good faith, as does lack of diligence and interference with or failure to cooperate in the other party's performance.[112] The government's violation of the implied duty to cooperate can amount to a material breach of contract.[113] The contractor may use this government breach both offensively in a claim for damages or defensively in an attempt to convert a termination for default to a termination for convenience. Consider the following examples:

Conversion of an improper default termination because of a failure to cooperate—In *Malone v. United States*,[114] the Air Force awarded Malone a contract to paint and refurbish houses. The contract required Malone to complete work on an initial house (the "exemplar") before commencing work on the remaining houses in order to demonstrate Malone's workmanship standards. Malone prepared and painted the exemplar, which the CO inspected but did not

approve, stating that he wanted time to consider possible changes.

The parties reached a compromise whereby Malone would immediately go to work on the carports in 65 houses while the CO considered the changes. Malone, however, believed that the CO had accepted the exemplar and immediately after completing work on the carports, began work on the houses themselves. The CO contributed to Malone's perception that he had accepted the exemplar in two ways: first, by failing to object to Malone's continued performance even though the CO knew what Malone was doing, and second, by continuing to pay invoices for work performed by Malone.

Eventually, the CO informed Malone that he had not approved the exemplar and stopped payment. By this time, Malone had completed about 70 percent of the work under the contract using the exemplar as its workmanship standard. Malone refused to re-perform its previous work in accordance, despite the government's insistence. The government subsequently terminated the contract for default. After stating that Malone had a duty to perform in the face of a dispute, unless there was a material breach of contract by the government, the court held that the government had materially breached the contract with Malone. The court found that the CO had misled Malone and induced its reliance on the exemplar as a workmanship standard by making progress payments and by refusing to answer Malone's explicit questions concerning whether the standard of workmanship had changed. The CO's evasive conduct led Malone to perform roughly 70 percent of its contractual obligations while relying on the workmanship standard that the CO later found unacceptable. The default termination was converted to one for the convenience of the government.

Damages for breach of duty to cooperate—In *Orlosky, Inc., v. United States*,[115] a contractor was able to recover the additional costs of an electrical project caused by the contracting agency's breach of its implied duty not to hinder performance and to cooperate. Here, the government did not cooperate in giving the contractor access to the site and granting the contractor's requests for power outages.

62

You failed to identify and submit a claim for a constructive change.

A constructive change entails two basic components: (1) the change component and (2) the order or fault component.[116] The change component describes work outside of the scope of the contract, while the order or fault component describes the reason that the contractor performed the work.[117] Therefore, if the government, either by express action or by implication, orders work outside the scope of the contract, or if the government otherwise requires the contractor to incur additional work, a constructive change arises for that work performed outside of the scope of the contract.[118] Where the government requires a constructive change, the government must fairly compensate the contractor for the costs of the change.[119]

Identifying what constitutes a constructive change can prove difficult, each case being highly fact-specific. The courts, however, have recognized five broad categories within which constructive changes tend to fall:

1. Disputes over contract interpretation during performance,

2. Government interference or failure to cooperate,

3. Defective specifications,

4. Misrepresentation and nondisclosure of superior knowledge, and

5. Acceleration of performance.[120]

Contractors must remain vigilant to ensure that they perform only as required by the text of their contract. When the government orders a contractor to deviate from the contract, the contractor should recognize the order as a constructive change and should notify the CO accordingly. This notification must be in writing and must request an equitable adjustment in the contract price or a modification to the delivery schedule, if necessary.

63

You failed to identify and submit a claim for defective specifications.

As mentioned earlier, defective specifications can amount to a constructive change, and a contractor may be entitled to an equitable adjustment for increased costs of performance due to the defective specifications.[121] Those claims arise where the specifications provided to the contractor by the government do not produce the end product that the government intended, and where the contractor is required to correct the problem.

If a contractor is required to build according to plans and specifications prepared by the government, then the contractor will not be responsible for the consequences of defects in those plans. That is, whenever the government uses specifications in a contract, there is an accompanying implied warranty that those specifications are free from errors,[122] and the government is bound to accept the result those specifications produce.[123] The test for a recovery that is based on inaccurate specifications is whether the contractor was misled by the errors.[124] If the contractor knew the specifications were inaccurate but built to those specifications anyway, it cannot recover.[125]

A note of caution—the warranty just referenced applies only to design specifications, not performance specifications. What is the difference?

- Design specifications describe in precise detail the materials to be used and the manner in which the work is to be performed. The contractor has no discretion to deviate from the specifications, and is required to follow them as a road map.[126]

- Performance specifications set forth an objective or standard to be achieved and the successful bidder is expected to exercise its ingenuity in achieving that objective or standard of performance, selecting the means, and assuming a corresponding responsibility for that selection.[127]

For example, design specification might be a blueprint for a vehicle, giving exact dimensions, weights, metals, etc. A performance specification for the same vehicle might simply say to "produce a vehicle that can carry four passengers of 200 pounds each at a top speed of 60 miles per hour on a paved road." The former is vulnerable to a charge of defective specifications; the latter is not.

64

You failed to recognize and claim impossibility of performance.

Although rare, sometimes it is impossible to perform a contract. Contractors need to understand that under certain conditions, their failure to perform will be excused. Contractors should assert their rights to nonperformance when this failure occurs.

A contractor has no duty to perform a contractual obligation if "performance is rendered impossible or impracticable, through no fault of the party, because of a fact, existing at the time the contract was made, of which the party neither knew nor had reason to know and the non-existence of which was a basic assumption of the party's agreement."[128] For the nonperformance of a contractual obligation to be excused by the doctrine of impossibility, the nonperforming party must show all of the following:

- A supervening event made performance impossible,

- The nonoccurrence of the event was a basic assumption on which the contract was based,

- The occurrence of the event was not the nonperforming party's fault, and

- The nonperforming party did not assume the risk of occurrence.[129]

The failure to perform must be objective, rather than subjective; that is, the duty at issue must be impossible for anyone to perform, not just the particular contractor who claims the excuse.[130]

The circumstances resulting in impossibility are rare, and the defense is a difficult one to maintain.

However, some impossibility defenses have been successful. Consider the following examples:

- In *Foster Wheeler Corp. v. United States*,[131] Foster-Wheeler agreed to provide shock-resistant marine boilers to the Navy. After Foster-Wheeler was unsuccessful, Foster-Wheeler was able to show that, given the design parameters agreed to by both parties, not only could it not produce the boilers with the necessary level of shock resistance, but also that no one could fabricate such a boiler. The court held that the contract was impossible to perform and that the government bore the risk of impossibility. Therefore, Foster-Wheeler was entitled to recover an equitable adjustment—pursuant to the changes clause—of costs incurred in attempting to meet the impossible specifications.

- In *Dynalectron Corp. (Pacific Division) v. United States*,[132] the court held that a contractor could not perform a contract for high-frequency antennas because the specifications were defective. The default termination was held improper, but the court ordered that the contractor and the government were "to share equally the allowable and reasonable costs normally recoverable by plaintiff in a convenience termination" because of careless contracting and contributory errors of the contractor.

- In *Suffolk Envtl. Magnetics, Inc.*,[133] although impossibility of performance was established (i.e., the perpendicularity of a bearing in the specifications was impossible to achieve), a termination for default was upheld because the contractor failed to provide the government with sufficient notice of the basis for the impossibility during the contractor's performance of the contract.

65

You failed to assert your right to an excusable delay.

Where a contractor is delayed for reasons that are not caused by its own fault or negligence and is, therefore, unable to complete or deliver a contract on time, the contractor should assert its right to an excusable delay and should insist that damages or default is inappropriate.

The excusable delay clause[134] states the following:

> Except for defaults of subcontractors at any tier, the [c]ontractor shall not be in default because of any failure to perform this contract under its terms if the failure arises from causes beyond the control and without the fault or negligence of the [c]ontractor. Examples of these causes are (1) acts of God or of the public enemy, (2) acts of the [g]overnment in either its sovereign or contractual capacity, (3) fires, (4) floods, (5) epidemics, (6) quarantine restrictions, (7) strikes, (8) freight embargoes, and (9) unusually severe weather. In each instance, the failure to perform must be beyond the control and without the fault or negligence of the [c]ontractor. "Default" includes failure to make progress in the work so as to endanger performance.

This clause, with respect to subcontractors, also states:

> b. If the failure to perform is caused by the failure of a subcontractor at any tier to perform or make progress, and if the cause of the failure was beyond the control of both the [c]ontractor and subcontractor, and [was] without the fault or negligence of either, the [c]ontractor shall not be deemed to be in default, unless—
>
> 1. The subcontracted supplies or services were obtainable from other sources;

2. The [c]ontracting [o]fficer ordered the [c]ontractor in writing to purchase these supplies or services from the other source; and

3. The [c]ontractor failed to comply reasonably with this order.

c. Upon request of the [c]ontractor, the [c]ontracting [o]fficer shall ascertain the facts and extent of the failure. If the [c]ontracting [o]fficer determines that any failure to perform results from one or more of the causes above, the delivery schedule shall be revised, subject to the rights of the [g]overnment under the termination clause of this contract.

Both Contract Terms and Conditions—Commercial Items[135] and Terms and Conditions—Simplified Acquisitions (Other Than Commercial Items)[136] include similar language.

A contractor who is terminated for default is entitled to a conversion of the default termination into one for the convenience of the government if the contractor can establish excusable delay.[137] The burden of proof of establishing excusable delay is on the contractor,[138] and the contractor must establish excusable delay by a preponderance of the evidence.[139] Also, where a contractor is delayed for excusable reason, liquidated damages should not be assessed.[140]

The meaning of these clauses is clear—if a contractor is delayed through no fault of its own, the delay is excusable and the government cannot assess damages or terminate the contract for default. Contractors should keep careful records of all excusable delays in the event the contractor should later need to meet its burden of proof. Also note that, if the delay is due to the fault of the government, not only will the contractor have a defense to a termination for default, but the contractor will also have a counterclaim

for an equitable adjustment on the basis of a constructive change. See the previous discussion of constructive change.

66

You failed to realize that the government may inspect at any reasonable place and time.

Contractors are well-advised not to object to government inspections unless the inspections unreasonably hinder contract performance. The standard inspection clause—the inspection of supplies fixed price clause,[141]—states:

The [g]overnment has the right to inspect and test all supplies called for by the contract, to the extent practicable, at all places and times, including the period of manufacture, and in any event before acceptance. The [g]overnment shall perform inspections and tests in a manner that will not unduly delay the work. The [g]overnment assumes no contractual obligation to perform any inspection and test for the benefit of the [c]ontractor unless specifically set forth elsewhere in this contract.

Contractors are usually unsuccessful in objecting to government inspections.

The government has several advantages in the rulings surrounding inspections. First, preproduction sample inspections and approval are acceptable. In *Comspace Corp.*,[142] Comspace appealed its termination for default for untimely performance, arguing that it was hindered in performing a contract for cable cord assemblies because the government made a "major change in the contract scope" by requiring approval of a preproduction sample as a prerequisite to delivery of the supplies. When Comspace previously provided this preproduction sample, the government (properly) rejected it and required a second and third sample, which Comspace later cited as justification for its untimely performance.

The board rejected Comspace's argument, citing the language of the Inspection of Supplies—Fixed Price clause previously discussed. The board held that the government had "the right to conduct any tests it deems reasonably necessary to ensure that the supplies or services conform in all respects to the contract specifications" and concluded that the government "had ample authority under the contract to conduct reasonable inspections of the cable cord assemblies prior to accepting them to ensure that they conformed to the drawings and specifications."[143]

Second, contractors may not demand that inspections occur at a particular place and time. A contractor asserted that it was improperly obligated to correct certain punch list items before the government accepted the project. The board found that the contract's inspection and acceptance clause gave the government the right to inspect all of the appellant's work "at all reasonable times and at all places prior to acceptance." The clause also required the appellant to "without charge, replace any material or correct any workmanship found…not to conform to the contract requirements."[144] The board noted that the appellant's unilateral declaration that the project was substantially completed had no effect on the government's inspection rights.[145]

Third and finally, the government is not obliged to inspect materials before installation. In *Ralph Larsen & Son, Inc.*,[146] the contractor asserted that the government was remiss in not inspecting contracted-for pipe before the pipe's installation. The board held:

> To adopt such a contention would negate [the contractor's] responsibility to perform its contract in accordance with the designated plans and specifications and [would] shift the risk of incurring

added costs for defective performance from [the contractor] to [the government]. The contract's [i]nspection and [a]cceptance provision required [the government] to inspect only at reasonable times, and it places all risk for deviation from the contract requirements on [the contractor]. Inspection prior to installation was not required of [the government].

67

You failed to take appropriate action to prevent a termination for default after the government properly rejected your tendered goods.

Where a contractor tenders nonconforming goods to the government, which the government subsequently and properly rejects, the contractor may be able to avoid a termination for default under at least two scenarios.

The first scenario occurs when the contractor tenders the goods before the delivery date specified in the contract, and the goods are thus rejected. The default clause states that the "[g]overnment may…terminate this contract in whole or in part if the [c]ontractor fails to [d]eliver the supplies or to perform the services within the time specified in this contract or any extension…."[147] Thus, the contractor is entitled to the full delivery period to correct any nonconformity and to tender conforming goods. Contractors should take advantage of their remaining time and should use all available resources to correct and deliver the goods on time. Keeping the severe consequences of a default termination in mind, consider using overtime or employing a subcontractor, if necessary, to complete the work in a timely manner. If the contractor can provide conforming goods before the delivery deadline in the contract, the government cannot default the contractor.

The second scenario occurs where the contractor has tendered goods that are in substantial but not total compliance. Under *Radiation Tech., Inc., v. United States*,[148] a contractor is entitled to a reasonable time to cure the nonconformities where an unexpected rejection occurs. A termination for default is inappropriate where the contractor can show all of the following:

- The supplies were delivered by the due date,

- The contractor had a reasonable belief that the supplies conformed to the contract requirements, and

- The defects were minor in nature and readily correctable.[149]

A good example of the application of the substantial compliance doctrine is in *Products Eng'g. Corp. v. General Servs. Admin.*[150] The company was awarded a contract for the procurement of combination squares (a type of woodworking tool). The contractor delivered its initial lots by the due date. The shipment was inspected by the contractor with the instruments customarily used by the contractor and was found to be acceptable. Although the contractor had no prior reason to anticipate that a coordinate measuring machine (CMM) would be used to test the combination squares, the government sent 13 squares off for CMM testing. Of the 13 squares, 5 squares were rejected for failing the length of blade requirement under the specifications. The discrepancy identified was minor in light of the contract's allowances for substantial deviation from the given specification, and the discrepancy was readily correctable. Accordingly, the substantial compliance doctrine applied, and the government (which had previously defaulted the contractor) was not allowed to collect excess reprocurement costs.

68

You failed to realize that the government can accept goods that are useable but that do not pass inspection if you can reach an agreement on a price reduction.

What can a contractor do when the goods or services it tenders to the government fail to meet the government's specifications? Is nonacceptance or even partial default the only answer? Although the government is entitled to strict compliance with the contract,[151] the government may agree to accept nonconforming materials and services, provided it obtains a price reduction.[152]

The standard supply contract inspection clause implies that the government may take a price reduction for nonconforming goods, should it choose to do so. The clause states:

> If acceptance is not conclusive…the [g]overnment, [may] require the [c]ontractor…to repay such portion of the contract as is equitable under the circumstances if the [c]ontracting [o]fficer elects not to require correction or replacement.[153]

The inspection of services clause expresses a similar sentiment and states that if the services do not conform to contract requirements, the government may "reduce the contract price to reflect the reduced value of the services performed."[154]

If you are confronted with the rejection of nonconforming goods and are unable to correct them, ask the CO if he or she will accept the goods after a unit price reduction. This request will work only if the CO agrees that the goods are of use to the government, even though they do not meet specifications.

A good example of acceptance with a price reduction is found in *Southland Enters. v. United States*,[155] where the contractor built a bridge for the government. Upon completion of the bridge, the government discovered that the bridge was nonconforming—the deck of the bridge contained numerous depressions. The government allowed Southland to repair the nonconforming deck. The government estimated (and Southland could not present evidence otherwise) that Southland's method of repair had a lifespan of approximately seven years. The bridge's estimated lifespan was 50 years, necessitating seven repairs over the life of the bridge. However, in accordance with the contract, the government accepted the repairs at a reduction in the bridge's price.

69

You failed to assert a prior course of dealing that made otherwise unacceptable goods acceptable.

Sometimes when a contractor does not provide exactly what is required by the contract's specifications, but does so over an extended period of time, the nonconforming item or service will be acceptable as the standard for the contract on the basis of waiver or a prior course of dealing.

Consider the example of *Gresham & Co., Inc., v. United States*,[156] where a contractor received 46 contracts with the same specification for single-tank dishwashers from the DOD. After completing 30 of those contracts, and having the products accepted by the government, an audit disclosed that the dishwashing machines were not fitted with automatic detergent dispensers. The CO asserted that dispensers were required by the specifications (a matter that the contractor disputed) and directed that all future machine deliveries (i.e., those in the remaining six contracts) be equipped with automatic detergent dispensers. The contractor complied with the directive and requested an equitable adjustment under the changes clause, but the CO denied it.

The court allowed the equitable adjustment, stating that "[t]here can be no doubt that a contract requirement for the benefit of a party becomes dead if that party knowingly fails to exact its performance, over such an extended period, that the other side reasonably believes the requirement to be dead." Underlying their ruling, the court noted that the machines in all 46 contracts had the same specification, and under none of the contracts did the plaintiff supply the automatic detergent dispensers until required under the alleged change orders. Under such circumstances, the court found that a reasonable contractor would believe "that the [automatic detergent dispenser] specification requirement was dead or at least suspended."

70

You failed to set up a records management system that complies with FAR Part 4, and that provides for the appropriate destruction of records when they reach the end of their regulatory service life.

FAR Subpart 4.7 establishes the requirements for contractor retention of records generated pursuant to the audit clauses for sealed bidding and negotiated procurement.[157] The record retention requirements ensure records are available for audit while permitting contractors to dispose of those records after a prescribed period of time has passed. A contractor that fails to establish a records management system consistent with FAR Part 4.7 may keep requisite records for less than the prescribed period, may needlessly consume physical or virtual space with unneeded and outdated records, or both. Moreover, records held beyond the required regulatory holding period represent a potential liability in the event of a future audit or criminal investigation.[158]

Retention periods are calculated starting from the end of the fiscal year in which an entry is made charging or allocating a cost to a government contract or subcontract.[159] These periods include:

- Financial and cost accounting records must be retained for four years, except for labor cost distribution and petty cash records, which should be retained for two years.[160]

- Pay administration records, including payroll sheets and salaries and wages paid, must be retained for four years, except for clock cards, time and attendance records, and paid checks or receipts for services, which should be retained for two years.[161]

- Acquisition and supply records must be retained for four years, except store requisitions for materials, supplies, equipment, and services, which must be held for two years.[162]

Contractors should (1) have on hand a written policy regarding their records management system that demonstrates compliance with the FAR and that is available to the government for review, (2) keep a log of what records were destroyed and when they were destroyed, and (3) routinely execute that policy. This policy places the government on notice of the contractor's routine business practices regarding records management in the event of an audit or investigation.

Under no circumstances is a contractor permitted to destroy relevant documents during an ongoing audit or investigation, even if the prescribed holding time has expired. The contractor's written policy should clearly and unambiguously reflect

this fact. There is a difference between a well-articulated and executed records management program and the systematic destruction of evidence and obstruction of justice. *Do not* engage in the latter!

ENDNOTES

1. FAR 1.602-1.

2. See, for example, Dept. of Agriculture Acquisition Regulation 416.405-2; Dept. of State Acquisition Regulation 652.242-70.

3. FAR 2.101 (defining "contracting officer").

4. See FAR 1.602-1(a).

5. There have been a few exceptions to this rule, including courts finding that a non-CO had inherent authority to direct a certain action. Those exceptions are so infrequent that a contractor in the normal course of business should simply ignore them.

6. *Design and Production, Inc., v. United States*, 18 Cl. Ct. 168 (1989).

7. See FAR 14.201-1.

8. FAR 52.252-2.

9. *General Engg. & Mach. Works v. OKeefe*, 991 F.2d 775, 779 (Fed. Cir. 1993).

10. *G. L. Christian and Assocs. v. United States*, 312 F.2d 418, 425 (Ct. Cl. 1963).

11. *Spring St. Found., Inc.*, AGBCA No. 92-232-1, 94-2, BCA ¶ 26,737.

12. 835 F.2d 865 (Fed. Cir. 1987).

13. 835 F.2d at 868 (citing *SCM Corp. v. United States*, 595 F.2d 595, 598 [Ct. Cl. 1979]).

14. FAR 2.101 [emphasis added].

15. Id. [emphasis added].

16. FAR 43.103 (A supplemental agreement means a contract modification that is accomplished by the mutual action of the parties; see also FAR 2.101. The Standard Form 30 (SF 30), Amendment of Solicitation/Modification of Contract, must be used for both supplemental agreements and change orders.

17. FAR 46.101.

18. *Cascade Pac. Int'l. v. United States*, 773 F.2d 287, 291 (Fed. Cir. 1985).

19. FAR 52.249-8.

20. FAR 52.249-8(c).

21. *Lisbon Contractors, Inc., v. United States*, 828 F.2d 759, 765 (Fed. Cir. 1987).

22. FAR 52.209-5(a)(1)(ii).

23. 31 U.S.C. § 3901 et seq.

24. 31 U.S.C. § 3903(b)(2).

25. FAR 52.232-25.

26. 5 C.F.R. Part 1315.

27. 31 U.S.C. § 3901 et seq.; see also FAR Subpart 32.9 and FAR 52.232-25.

28. *N. Star Ala. Hous. Corp. v. United States*, 30 Fed. Cl. 259, 272 (1993) (citing *Calfon Constr. v. United States*, 17 Cl. Ct. 171, 177 (1989)).

29. FAR 52.222-43.

30. 457 F.3d 1262 (Fed. Cir. 2006).

31. See *Dynamics Corp. of Am. v. United States*, 389 F.2d 424, 431 (Ct. Cl.1968); *Government Sys. Advisors, Inc., v. United States*, 847 F.2d 811, 813 (Fed. Cir. 1988).

32. FAR 52.217-8.

33. FAR 52.232-19.

34. 31 U.S.C. § 1341(a).

35. Williston on Contracts § 61A (3d ed., 1957).

36. Williston on Contracts, supra, § 61B.

37. See, e.g., *Dynamics Corp. of Am. v. United States*, 389 F.2d 424 (Ct. Cl. 1968); *Contel Page Services, Inc.*, ASBCA No. 32100, 87-1 BCA ¶ 19,540.

38. See, e.g., *Moore's Cafeteria Servs. Inc.*, ASBCA No. 28441, 85-3 BCA ¶ 18,187; *Holly Corp.*, ASBCA No. 24975, 83-1 BCA ¶ 16,327; *Universal Am. Enterprises, Inc.*, ASBCA No. 22562, 81-1, BCA ¶ 14,942.

39. See, e.g., *J.E.T.S., Inc.*, ASBCA No. 26135, 82-2 BCA ¶ 15,986; *Gen. Dynamics Corp.*, ASBCA No. 20882, 77-1, BCA ¶ 12,504.

40. *White Sands Constr., Inc.*, ASBCA Nos. 51875, 54029, 04-1, BCA ¶ 32,598.

41. See *J.E.T.S., Inc.*, ASBCA No. 26135, 82-2, BCA ¶ 15,986.

42. FAR 52.232-18. The clause reads, in full, as follows:

> Funds are not presently available for this contract. The [g]overnment's obligation under this contract is contingent upon the availability of appropriated funds from which payment for contract purposes can be made. No legal liability on the part of the [g]overnment for any payment may arise until funds are made available to the [c]ontracting [o]fficer for this contract and until the [c]ontractor receives notice of such availability, to be confirmed in writing by the [c]ontracting [o]fficer.

43. FAR 52.222-6.

44. FAR 52.222-41.

45. FAR 52.222-6(b)(1).

46. FAR 52.222-41(l).

47. See, e.g., *Westchester Fire Ins. Co. v. United States*, 52 Fed. Cl. 567, 580 (2002) (funds withheld from prime contractor for subcontractor's wage violations).

48. 29 C.F.R. § 4.187 (Service Contract Act) and 29 C.F.R § 5.9 (Davis-Bacon Act).

49. 29 C.F.R. §4.188 (Service Contract Act) and 29 C.F.R. § 5.12 (Davis-Bacon Act).

50. 29 C.F.R. § 5.10(b) (Davis-Bacon Act).

51. 29 C.F.R. §4.190 (Service Contract Act).

52. Only Louisiana has not adopted U.C.C. Article 2. Even the District of Columbia and the Virgin Islands have adopted it.

53. UCC 2-209(1).

54. *United States v. Stump Home Specialties Mfg., Inc.*, 905 F.2d 1117, 1121 (7th Cir. 1990).

55. FAR 8.406-3.

56. DOTCAB No. 2928, 98-2, BCA ¶29,783.

57. DFARS 252.227-7013.

58. DFARS 252.227-7014.

59. DFARS 227.7103-5(b).

60. DFARS 252.227-7013(a)(13).

61. DFARS 227.7103-5 and DFARS 227.7203-5.

62. FAR 52.243-1.

63. 456 F.2d 760 (Ct. Cl. 1972).

64. See *Central Mech. Constr.*, ASBCA Nos. 29431, et al., 85-2,BCA ¶ 18,061.

65. See, e.g., id.; *Davis Decorating Serv.*, ASBCA No. 17342, 73-2 ,BCA ¶ 10,107.

66. See *Central Mech. Constr.*, ASBCA Nos. 29431, et al., 85-2, BCA ¶ 18,061.

67. LBCA No. 94-BCA-3, 98-2 BCA ¶ 30,007.

68. 41 U.S.C. § 605(b) (emphasis added).

69. FAR 52.233-1(i).

70. 178 F.3d 1260, 1277 (1999).

71. See *Malone v. United States*, 849 F.2d 1441, 1445 (Fed. Cir. 1988).

72. *Alliant Techsystems*, 178 F.3d at 1276.

73. *United States v. DeKonty Corp.*, 922 F 2d 826 (Fed. Cir. 1991).

74. *Cascade Pac. Int'l. v. United States*, 773 F.2d 287 (Fed. Cir. 1985).

75. Id.

76. CBCA No. 243, 07-2 BCA ¶ 33,598.

77. FAR 52.232-20.

78. FAR 52.232-22.

79. FAR 32.705-2.

80. FAR 52.232-20(b) (LOC); FAR § 52.232-22(c) (LOF).

81. See, e.g., *Advanced Materials, Inc., v. Perry*, 108 F.3d 307, 310 (Fed. Cir. 1997).

82. Id.

83. Id.; see also FAR 52.232-20(d)(1) (LOC); FAR 52.232-22(e) (LOF).

84. FAR 32.704.

85. 129 F.3d 1479, (Fed. Cir. 1997).

86. *Titan*, 129 F.3d at 1482.

87. 41 U.S.C. §§ 10a-d.

88. 19 U.S.C. 2501 et seq.

89. FAR 25.402.

90. *Glazer Const. Co., Inc., v. United States*, 52 Fed. Cl. 513 (2002).

91. 28 F.Supp. 2d 213 (D. N.J. 1998).

92. Id.

93. ASBCA No. 30025, 85-2 BCA 18077. See also *H & R Machinists Co.*, ASBCA No. 38440, 91-1 BCA ¶ 23,373 (appeal of termination for default because of BAA violations was not granted by ASBCA).

94. FAR 9.103.

95. FAR 9.104-1.

96. FAR 9.405.

97. FAR 9.405-1.

98. FAR 9.406-2.

99. See FAR. 9.407-2.

100. FAR 9.406-1.

101. FAR 9.402(b).

102. FAR 9.406-1(a).

103. Id.

104. 5 U.S.C. § 706(2).

105. 2007 WL 207179 (D.D.C. 2007) (slip op.).

106. A criminal information is a charging document similar to an indictment; however, it is signed by a prosecutor and not by a grand jury foreperson.

107. Id.

108. Id.

109. Id.

110. *Essex Electro Eng'rs., Inc., v. Danzig*, 224 F.3d 1283, 1291 (Fed. Cir. 2000) (quoting *Luria Bros. v. United States*, 369 F.2d 701, 708 (Ct. Cl. 1966)) (citations omitted).

111. See *Malone v. United States*, 849 F.2d 1441, 1445 (Fed. Cir. 1988).

112. Restatement (Second) of Contracts § 205 cmt. d (1981); see also *Tecom, Inc., v. United States*, 66 Fed. Cl. 736, 769 (2005) (stating that the implied duty to cooperate appears to be an aspect of "the overarching duty of good faith and fair dealing").

113. *Tecom, Inc., v. United States*, 66 Fed. Cl. 736, 771 (2005).

114. 849 F.2d 1441 (Fed. Cir. 1988).

115. 68 Fed. Cl. 296 (2005).

116. *Johnson Constr. Co. v. United States*, 20 Cl. Ct. 184, 204 (1990).

117. *Embassy Moving & Storage Co. v. United States*, 424 F.2d 602, 607 (Ct. Cl. 1970); *Eggers & Higgins & Edwin A. Keeble Assocs., Inc., v. United States*, 403 F.2d 225, 236 (Ct. Cl. 1968).

118. *Lathan Co. v. United States*, 20 Cl. Ct. 122, 128 (1990).

119. *Aydin Corp. v. Widnall*, 61 F.3d 1571, 1577 (Ct. Cl. 1971).

120. *Miller Elevator Co., Inc., v. United States*, 30 Fed. Cl. 662, 678 (1994).

121. *Clearwater Constructors, Inc., v. United States*, 71 Fed. Cl. 25, 32 (2006) (citing *L. W. Foster Sportswear Co. v. United States*, 405 F.2d 1285 (Ct. Cl. 1969)).

122. *United States v. Spearin*, 248 U.S. 132, 137 (1918).

123. See *PCL Const. Servs., Inc., v. United States*, 47 Fed. Cl. 745, 795 (2000).

124. For example, in *Wickham Contracting Co., Inc., v. United States*, 546 F.2d 395, 400-01 (Ct. Cl. 1976), the contractor based its bid on an erroneous scale in a contract drawing. When the government asked for verification of the plaintiff's bid, the plaintiff became aware of the error in scale. "Since plaintiff was aware of the drawing error at the time it entered into the contract, refusing an opportunity to withdraw its bid based on the drawing error, it is not entitled to recover additional costs by way of a contract price adjustment based on said error."

125. Id.

126. *Blake Constr. Co. v. United States*, 987 F.2d 743, 745 (Fed. Cir. 1993).

127. Id.

128. *Mass. Bay Transp. Auth. v. United States*, 254 F.3d 1367, 1372 (Fed. Cir. 2001).

129. *Seaboard Lumber Co. v. United States*, 308 F.3d 1283, 1294 (Fed. Cir. 2002).

130. *Int'l Electronics Corp. v. United States*, 646 F.2d 496, 510 (Ct. Cl. 1981).

131. 513 F.2d 588. (Ct. Cl. 1975).

132. 518 F.2d 594 (Ct. Cl. 1975).

133. ASBCA No. 17593, 74-2 BCA ¶ 10,771.

134. FAR 52.249-14.

135. FAR 52.212-4.

136. FAR 52.213-4.

137. FAR 54.249-9(g) states that "[i]f, after [default] termination, it is determined that the [c]ontractor was not in default, or that the default was excusable, the rights and obligations of the parties shall be the same as if the termination had been issued for the convenience of the [g]overnment."

138. *Arctic Corner, Inc.*, ASBCA No. 29405, 88-1 BCA ¶ 20,396.

139. *Mil-Craft Mfg.*, ASBCA 19305, 74-2 BCA ¶ 10,840.

140. *Sauer, Inc., v. Danzig*, 224 F. 3d 1340, 1347 (Fed. Cir. 2000).

141. FAR 52.246-2(c).

142. DOTCAB No. 4011, March 11, 2002, 2002 WL 378322.

143. Id.

144. *BECO Corp.*, ASBCA No. 27296, 83-2 BCA ¶ 16,724.

145. Id.

146. PSBCA No. 2038, 88-3 BCA ¶ 20,940.

147. FAR 52.249-8(a)(1).

148. 366 F.2d 1003 (Ct. Cl. 1966).

149. Id. at 1005-06.

150. GSBCA No. 13051, 98-2 BCA ¶ 29,851.

151. *Teg-Paradigm Envtl., Inc., v. United States*, 465 F.3d 1329, 1342 (Fed. Cir. 2006).

152. *Farwell Co. v. United States*, 148 F. Supp. 947 (Ct. Cl. 1957).

153. FAR 52.246-2(l).

154. FAR 52.246-4(e).

155. 24 Cl. Ct. 596 (1991).

156. 470 F.2d 542 (Ct. Cl. 1972).

157. FAR 52.214-26, Audit and Records—Sealed Bidding, and FAR 52.215-2, Audit and Records—Negotiation.

158. Auditors and criminal investigators generally obtain records from a contractor, even when a contracting agency is required to keep identical records. If the contractor is no longer required to maintain the records and has disposed of them, then there is likely to be no resulting audit or criminal investigation.

159. FAR 4.704.

160. FAR 4.705-1.

161. FAR 4.705-2.

162. FAR 4.705-3.

Chapter 9

Contract Pricing and Costs

71

You failed to demonstrate to an auditor or cost and price analyst that the price in your offer was reasonable.

In a cost reimbursement contract, a contractor's cost estimate must be both reasonable and supportable. In support of this goal, agencies are required to conduct a cost reasonableness analysis in all competitions for cost reimbursement contracts. Because FAR Part 31 requires agencies to pay actual and allowable costs once an award is made—regardless of the offeror's proposal—the analysis must determine if the proposed cost is a reasonable estimate of what will be the actual cost.[1] Each element of the offeror's cost estimate will be scrutinized to determine if the proposed costs are realistic for the work to be performed, if the costs indicate a clear understanding of the requirements, and if they are consistent with the methods of performance and materials described in the offeror's proposal.[2] If a contractor's proposal fails to stand up under this review and appears unreasonably low, the agency will revise the proposal upward in price,[3] thus reducing that contractor's chance of winning the award. Agencies are imperfect, and their analyses are sometimes unreasonable. Consider the following examples:

Improper adjustment by agency of indirect cost—An agency's removal of program management costs from an awardee's proposed indirect costs during its cost realism analysis is unreasonable where inclusion of such costs is consistent with current cost accounting standards and practices.[4]

Improper treatment of team members' cost—Where an offeror proposed to perform under a teaming arrangement, the Government Accountability Office (GAO) held the agency's cost realism analysis was unreasonable when the analysis failed to consider the effect of the offeror's team members' labor rates in determining the offeror's probable cost of performance. The GAO recommended that the agency hold discussions to more accurately gauge the effect of the proposed teaming agreement on the offeror's actual costs and to reevaluate the proposals accordingly.[5]

Unreasonable treatment of uncompensated overtime—In a solicitation for a cost reimbursement contract where the use of uncompensated overtime was not prohibited, an agency unreasonably raised the offeror's proposed costs in its cost realism analysis when it eliminated the effect of the offeror's proposed use of uncompensated overtime.[6]

72

Your proposal or invoices included unallowable costs.

Contractors must scrupulously avoid including unallowable costs in their contract proposals, invoices, or any other document used to later support a request for funds from the government. Unallowable costs are costs that, "under the provisions of any pertinent law, regulation, or contract, cannot be included in prices, cost-reimbursements, or settlements under a [g]overnment contract to which it is allocable."[7]

Costs are allowable under government contracts in accordance with Part 31 of the *FAR*, which states that such a cost must be (1) reasonable; (2) allocable to the contracts; (3) consistent with standards promulgated by the Cost Accounting Standards Board, if applicable—otherwise, consistent with generally accepted accounting principles and practices appropriate to the circumstances; (4) consistent with all terms of the contract; and (5) within any limitations set forth in FAR Subpart 31.2.[8]

There are special provisions in the *FAR* for indirect costs. The *FAR* states that "[i]f unallowable costs are included in final indirect cost settlement proposals, penalties may be assessed."[9] Those penalties are outlined in FAR 42.709 and can be severe. FAR 42.709-1 states:

a. The following penalties apply to contracts covered by this section:

1. If the indirect cost is expressly unallowable under a cost principle in the *FAR*, or an executive agency supplement to the *FAR*, that defines the allowability of specific selected costs, the penalty is equal to—

    i. The amount of the disallowed costs allocated to contracts that are subject to this section for which an indirect cost proposal has been submitted; plus

    ii. Interest on the paid portion, if any, of the disallowance.

2. If the indirect cost was determined to be unallowable for that contractor before proposal submission, the penalty is two times the amount in paragraph (a)(1)(i) of this section.

    i. These penalties are in addition to other administrative, civil, and criminal penalties provided by law.

    ii. It is not necessary for unallowable costs to have been paid to the contractor in order to assess a penalty.

ENDNOTES

1. See FAR 15.305(a)(1) and 15.404-1(d)(1),(2).

2. FAR 15.404-1(d)(1).

3. See FAR 15.404-1(d)(2)(ii).

4. *Kellogg Brown & Root Servs., Inc.*, B-298694, Nov. 16, 2006, 2006 WL 3411093.

5. *Metro Machine Corp.*, B-297879.2, May 3, 2006, 2006 CPD ¶ 80.

6. *SRS Techs.*, B-291618.2, Feb. 24, 2003, 2003 CPD ¶ 70.

7. FAR 2.101 (defining "unallowable costs").

8. See, generally, FAR Part 31.

9. FAR 31.110(b).

Chapter 10

Government Furnished Property

73

You failed to maintain a proper inventory of government furnished property.

Contractors are responsible for maintaining a viable property management system, which accounts for all government furnished property (GFP). The property management system should reflect all transactions involving the gain or loss of GFP and should provide a current, auditable inventory of GFP at all times. Periodic physical inventories of GFP are required as well. Finally, the contractor must ensure that its subcontractors maintain a similar system for GFP.[1] The absence of such a system may result in revocation of the government's assumption of risk for loss, damage, destruction, or theft of GFP.[2] Because GFP may be quite valuable, maintenance of a property management system is essential.

74

You failed to request an equitable adjustment when the government did not meet its obligations with respect to government furnished property.

Although the contractor is accountable for GFP once conveyed into its possession, the government is responsible for ensuring the GFP is provided to the contractor on time and in good working order.[3] Furthermore, if the government delivers the GFP in a condition not suitable for its intended use, the government is responsible for remedying the problem. The remedy may include repairing, replacing, modifying, returning, or disposing of the property—all at the government's expense. A contractor is owed an equitable adjustment when the government fails to meet those obligations.[4] Consider the following examples:

GFP not suitable for intended use and replaced by contractor—In *W. States Mgmt. Servs., Inc.*,[5] the government was required to furnish a custodial contractor with certain equipment and supplies that were suitable to place a "uniform glossy finish" on the floors of a military commissary. The property furnished was unable to achieve the required finish, and the contractor replaced the defective GFP to achieve the required finish. The board granted the contractor the cost of replacing the defective equipment because the GFP was not suitable for its intended purpose.

GFP provided late—In a contract awarded by the Army and Air Force Exchange Service (AAFES) for the production of trousers, the government was responsible for supplying the requisite fabric. The government's fabric supplier encountered production problems and was unable to supply any acceptable fabric to the contractor during a 14-month period. In view of the fabric problem, AAFES stopped issuing delivery orders to the contractor. Because the contractor could not find additional work to mitigate its lost production capacity, the contractor was entitled to an equitable adjustment.[6]

ENDNOTES

1. FAR 52.245-1.

2. FAR 45.105(b). Note that FAR 52.245-1(h) indicates that the contractor is not liable for loss, damage, destruction, or theft of GFP except when the risk is covered by insurance, the loss results from willful misconduct or lack of good faith of the contractor, or the contracting officer has revoked the government's assumption of risk as stated earlier.

3. FAR 52.245-1(d).

4. FAR 52.245-1(d)(2)(i).

5. ASBCA No. 40546, 92-1 BCA ¶ 24,753.

6. *Finesilver Mfg. Co.*, ASBCA No. 28955, 86-3 BCA ¶ 19,243.

Chapter 11

Contract Termination

75

You failed to properly respond to a cure notice or show-cause notice.

To a government contractor, the receipt of a cure notice or a show-cause notice is akin to a four-alarm fire. The contractor must take quick, decisive action, or the damage may be irreparable. These notices are used (1) to inform a contractor that the agency believes there are reasons its contract should be defaulted and (2) to give the contractor an opportunity either to cure the default or to explain why a default termination should not be made. A contractor should respond fully, forcefully, and with clear and convincing evidence so it can avoid a default.

The default (fixed-price supply and service) clause states:

1. The [g]overnment may...by written notice of default to the [c]ontractor, terminate this contract in whole or in part if the [c]ontractor fails to

    i. Deliver the supplies or to perform the services within the time specified in this contract or any extension;

    ii. Make progress, so as to endanger performance of this contract...; or

    iii. Perform any of the other provisions of this contract...

2. The [g]overnment's right to terminate this contract under subdivisions (1)(ii) and (1)(iii) above, may be exercised if the [c]ontractor does not cure such failure within 10 days (or more if authorized in writing by the [c]ontracting [o]fficer) after receipt of the notice from the [c]ontracting [o]fficer specifying the failure.[1]

The form of a cure notice is given in the *FAR*:

> Cure Notice: You are notified that the [g]overnment considers your...[specify the contractor's failure or failures] a condition that is endangering performance of the contract. Therefore, unless this condition is cured within 10 days after receipt of this notice [or insert any longer time that the contracting officer may consider reasonably necessary], the [g]overnment may terminate for default under the terms and conditions of the...[insert clause title] clause of this contract.[2]

As you can see, a cure notice indicates that the contracting officer (CO) believes a default termination is appropriate and imminent, unless the contractor corrects the deficiency or furnishes clear and convincing evidence that the deficiency is through no fault of the contractor. In those circumstances, assistance of legal counsel should be considered. More important, the contractor must respond to the cure notice immediately.

Note that no cure notice is required where the contractor fails to deliver supplies on time. The contractor may be terminated immediately upon written notice.

The *FAR* indicates that if termination for default appears appropriate, the CO should, if practicable, notify the contractor in writing of the possibility of the termination through the issuance of a show-cause notice. However, a show-cause notice is not mandatory. FAR 49.402-3(e)(1) describes a show-cause notice as follows:

> This notice shall call the contractor's attention to the contractual liabilities if the contract is terminated for default, and request the contractor to show cause why the contract should not be terminated for default. The notice may further state that failure of the contractor to present an

explanation may be taken as an admission that no valid explanation exists. When appropriate, the notice may invite the contractor to discuss the matter at a conference.

The *FAR* specifies the following format for a show-cause notice:

> Show-Cause Notice: Since you have failed to…[insert "perform Contract No…within the time required by its terms," or "cure the conditions endangering performance under Contract No…as described to you in the [g]overnment's letter of…(date)"], the [g]overnment is considering terminating the contract under the provisions for default of this contract. Pending a final decision in this matter, it will be necessary to determine whether your failure to perform arose from causes beyond your control and without fault or negligence on your part. Accordingly, you are given the opportunity to present, in writing, any facts bearing on the question to…[insert the name and complete address of the contracting officer], within 10 days after receipt of this notice. Your failure to present any excuses within this time may be considered as an admission that none exist. Your attention is invited to the respective rights of the [c]ontractor and the [g]overnment and the liabilities that may be invoked if a decision is made to terminate for default.[3]

Any contractor who receives a show-cause notice should again make a substantial and convincing written argument to the CO as to why the default is inappropriate. The response should also request a meeting with the CO to see if the matter can be resolved without a default.

76

You failed to challenge an improper termination for default.

A termination for default results in the loss of the current contract and possibly the loss of future contracts. Therefore, a government contractor must contest any improper default termination, including an appeal to a board or to the Court of Federal Claims, if necessary. If the contractor can show that the default termination was improper, it will be converted to a termination for convenience,[4] a vastly superior outcome for the contractor.

There are several reasons a default termination may be improper, including the following:

- The facts demonstrate that the contractor was not actually in default.

- Any failure to perform arose from causes beyond the control and without the fault or negligence of the contractor, such as acts of God or the public enemy, acts of the government in either its sovereign or contractual capacity, fires, floods, epidemics, quarantine restrictions, strikes, freight embargoes, and unusually severe weather.[5]

- The facts show any other reason the contractor's failure to perform was beyond the control of the contractor and not due to the fault or negligence of the contractor.[6]

- Failure to perform was caused by government actions or inactions. The government may not do anything to prevent performance by the contractor that will hinder or delay the contractor in its performance.[7] Not only must the government refrain from hindering the contractor's performance, but also it must do whatever is reasonably necessary to enable the contractor to perform.[8]

Under a termination for default, the government is not liable for unaccepted work.[9] It pays only for work that has been accepted. The government is also entitled to reprocure the supplies or services from another source and to charge the contractor the excess costs of reprocurement.[10] For example, if the new contract is awarded at $1.5 million, and the defaulted contract was priced at $1 million, the defaulted contractor will owe the government the excess cost of reprocurement, or $500,000. However, the government must procure the same or similar supplies and has a duty to mitigate the damages. In a termination for default, the contractor is also required to return any advance payments or progress payments.

Even more significant than the immediate financial effect of a default termination is the effect on future responsibility and past performance evaluations. To be deemed "presently responsible" and eligible for contract award, a contractor must have a satisfactory performance record.[11] Contractors are required to certify as to whether they have suffered a default termination during the past three years.[12] The *FAR* indicates that a contractor that is, or has recently been,

> seriously deficient in contract performance
> shall be presumed to be nonresponsible, unless
> the contracting officer determines that the
> circumstances were properly beyond the contractor's
> control or that the contractor has taken appropriate
> corrective actions…[T]he contracting officer shall
> consider the number of contracts involved and the
> extent of deficient performance in each contract
> when making this determination.[13]

A default termination represents a seriously deficient performance by a contractor. Although one default termination left unchallenged may be explainable, it is unlikely that two or more defaults can be explained. In the event of two or more unchallenged terminations for default, not only will the contractor likely be deemed nonresponsible,

but also it may be suspended or debarred pursuant to FAR Subpart 9.1. By challenging improper default terminations, the contractor has the ability to explain a situation to a CO on a contract on which it competes. It is strongly suggested that a contractor provide a full explanation concerning any default and any appeals taken with respect to default in its certification in FAR 52.209-5.

Finally, a default termination will negatively affect a contractor's past performance evaluations when competing for subsequent contract awards. Past performance evaluations are required in all negotiated procurements over $100,000.[14] The *FAR* states that "[w]hen selecting contractors to provide products or perform services, the [g]overnment will use contractors who have a track record of successful past performance or who demonstrate a current superior ability to perform."[15] Here is how the *FAR* suggests that past performance be evaluated:

i. Past performance information is one indicator of an offeror's ability to perform the contract successfully. The currency and relevance of the information, source of the information, context of the data, and general trends in contractor's performance shall be considered. This comparative assessment of past performance information is separate from the responsibility determination required under subpart 9.1.

ii. The solicitation shall describe the approach for evaluating past performance, including evaluating offerors with no relevant performance history, and shall provide offerors an opportunity to identify past or current contracts (including [f]ederal, [s]tate, and local government and private) for efforts similar to the [g]overnment requirement. The solicitation shall also authorize offerors to provide information on problems encountered on the identified contracts and the offeror corrective actions. The [g]overnment shall consider this information, as well as information obtained from any other sources, when evaluating the offeror['s] past performance. The source selection authority shall determine the relevance of similar past performance information.[16]

A default termination is a big black mark on subsequent past performance evaluations, may result in a finding of nonresponsibility, and will result in an immediate financial loss for the contractor on the current contract. Because default terminations carry such grave consequences, contractors must challenge any improper default. The counsel of an experienced government contracts attorney is advised.

77

You endangered the performance of your contract.

Actions taken by a contractor (or lack thereof) that prospectively place the delivery schedule, or any other aspect of the contract, in jeopardy are actions that endanger contract performance. Under such circumstances, the government may properly terminate the contract for default.[17] A few examples will demonstrate this principle:

Contractor failed to provide an adequate schedule—In a contract to build campgrounds in a National Park, the contractor was properly defaulted because it failed to make adequate progress, did not assure the government of timely delivery, and did not submit a project schedule. The lack of an adequate schedule indicated that the contractor was not ready, willing, or able to make progress, and also supported the government's position that it was justifiably insecure about the contract's timely completion.[18]

Contractor had no completion plan or strategy—In a construction contract to build a post office, the contractor had completed only 10 percent of the work after seven months on the project and had numerous problems and delays in bidding out subcontractors. The contractor failed to respond to the government's concerns and, despite repeated requests from the U.S. Postal Service, did not provide an adequate schedule or an overall completion plan or strategy. It was reasonable for the Postal Service to believe that performance was endangered.[19]

Contractor had 60 days of work to perform in three days—In a construction contract for campgrounds, the government justifiably terminated the contract for default where only three days remained before the contract's completion date and at least 60 days worth of work remained, despite 80 percent of the work being completed as of the termination date.[20]

When a contract's delivery schedule begins to tighten, and you realize that timely performance may be impossible, don't wait for the inevitable. Contact the CO, and discuss the possibility of obtaining modification. Although default terminations affect contractors the most, the government doesn't escape unscathed. The government will likely be forced to recompete the contract, which costs both money and time. Explain your situation and your reasons for the delay. Assure the CO that you can meet a revised delivery schedule. With any luck, if you identify and correct the deficiency early enough, the CO will agree to the modification.

78

You failed to assert that the government waived the delivery schedule when it sought to default you after substantial time had passed for delivery or performance.

If the government waives a delivery date, a contractor may have an important defense to any subsequent termination for default. If the government elects to permit a delinquent contractor to continue performance past a contract completion date, it waives its contractual right to terminate for default if the contractor has not abandoned performance and if a reasonable time has elapsed for issuance of a termination notice. It is not clear exactly how much time must elapse, but a failure to terminate within a week or two is likely to result in a waiver. There are two elements to the government's waiver of the default: (1) a failure to terminate within a reasonable time after the default, under circumstances indicating forbearance, and (2) the contractor relying on that failure and continuing to perform the contract with the government's knowledge and implied or express consent. Once a performance date has passed and the contract has not been terminated for default within a reasonable time, time does not again become "of the essence" until the government issues a notice that sets a new timeline for performance, which is both specific and reasonable from the standpoint of the contractor.

An example of the government's waiver of the delivery schedule is found in *Technocratica*,[21] where the government terminated a contract for the construction of a racquetball court at a U.S. Navy installation in Souda Bay, Greece. The contract specified completion by July 24, 1993. Leading up to the completion date, the Navy sent several letters expressing its concern over the lack of timely progress (e.g., "work is [four percent]

complete, while 42 [percent] of the time has elapsed"; "23 [percent] of the work is complete, while 88 [percent] of the time has elapsed").[22] Ultimately, the Navy gave the contractor a 10-day cure notice on July 1, 1993.

Four days after the completion date, with the racquetball court unfinished, the Navy issued a show-cause letter, asking whether Technocratica's failure to perform was due to circumstances beyond its control, or whether it was due to Technocratica's own negligence. Shortly thereafter, a local CO recommended a termination for default. However, the Navy's Chief of Contracts for the Mediterranean Area—the only contracting official authorized to default the contract—declined to do so. Instead, the official elected to let Technocratica "muddle through a little bit longer and [to] see how things went."[23] Technocratica continued to perform, while the Navy began a written discourse with the company about the specific requirements of the project and revised schedules. This conduct demonstrated that the Navy knew that Technocratica had not performed on time and expressly consented to Technocratica's continued performance.

Finally, on September 1, 1994, 13 months after the completion date, the Navy terminated the contract for default with the racquetball court's construction still incomplete. The Armed Services Board of Contract Appeals (ASBCA) deemed the default improper and converted it to a termination for the convenience of the government. The ASBCA found both of the previously stated elements were present to find a governmental election to waive default.

Where the delivery date has been waived, any default must be converted to a termination for the convenience of the government, the contractor will receive no black mark on its performance record, and it will be eligible for a termination for convenience settlement.[24]

79

Upon receipt of a valid default, you failed to contest the government's unreasonable excess cost of reprocurement.

Among the numerous problems that arise for a contractor after a termination of default is the contractor's liability for the government's excess costs of reprocurement. Although this liability is likely to be onerous, it needn't be unreasonably so. The Federal Circuit Court has stated:

> [E]xcess reprocurement costs may be imposed only when the [g]overnment meets its burden of persuasion that the following conditions (factual determinations) are met: (1) the reprocured supplies are the same as or similar to those involved in the termination, (2) the [g] overnment actually incurred excess costs, and (3) the [g]overnment acted reasonably to minimize the excess costs resulting from the default. The first condition is demonstrated by comparing the item reprocured with the item specified in the original contract. The second condition requires the [g]overnment to show what it spent in reprocurement. The third condition requires that the [g]overnment act within a reasonable time of the default, use the most efficient method of reprocurement, obtain a reasonable price, and mitigate its losses.[25]

The CO has great discretion in any reprocurement. However, it is not unfettered. A CO has a duty to act within a reasonable time after default, to obtain a reasonable price, and to mitigate the contractor's damages.[26] What constitutes a reasonable time depends on the facts and circumstances that exist in a particular situation, but the test is usually whether the contractor was charged a higher price because of the passage of time.[27]

Although competition is not explicitly required, the court and boards deem some type of competition essential. As the decision in *Camrex Reliance Paint Co.*[28] explains:

> To obtain adequate competition in the reprocurement, offers must be solicited from a sufficient number of competent potential sources to ensure adequate competition. The [g]overnment is not required, however, to solicit every known source of supply; nor is it required to solicit all who bid on the original solicitation. Where there is no reason to believe that solicitation of a greater number of potential contractors would have resulted in lower prices, the [g]overnment will be found to have fulfilled its duty to mitigate damages.

Where contractors find a violation of any of these principles, they should act within the time limits for an appeal on any assessment of excess cost of reprocurement.

80

You failed to request a no-cost termination in lieu of a default termination.

This book has already discussed at length the significant negative effect of a default termination on a contractor, including future responsibility determinations, past performance evaluations, increased potential for suspension or debarment, financial hit from the loss of the instant contract, and liability for the excess cost of reprocurement. A contractor who has received a cure notice, or is otherwise facing a potential default, should attempt to negotiate a no-cost termination that excludes the default component and avoids the litany of woes that accompany it. The *FAR* specifically sanctions alternatives to default terminations, including the no-cost termination, as follows:

> The following courses of action, among others, are available to the contracting officer in lieu of termination for default when in the [g]overnment's interest:

a. Permit the contractor, the surety, or the guarantor, to continue performance of the contract under a revised delivery schedule.

b. Permit the contractor to continue performance of the contract by means of a subcontract or other business arrangement with an acceptable third party, provided the rights of the [g]overnment are adequately preserved.

c. If the requirement for the supplies and services in the contract no longer exists, and [if] the contractor is not liable to the [g]overnment for [excess cost of reprocurement or other administrative costs], execute a no-cost termination settlement.[29]

Two specific no-cost settlement agreements are provided at FAR 49.603-6 and FAR 49.603-7. Each provides for a condition that permits the contractor to demand a waiver of the excess cost of reprocurement. Sometimes a no-cost settlement can be achieved merely through a modification to the contract that "ends performance as of the date of modification and appropriately modifies the statement of work or delivery schedule so that it ends coincident with the modification." This is another form of settlement that can effectively dispense with the excess cost of reprocurement.

When the government defaults a contractor, the government bears the burden of proof in justifying the default.[30] A contractor should gently remind the CO of this burden, while laying out its case for a no-cost termination.

COs may be willing to enter a no-cost settlement where:

- The requirement for supplies or services no longer exists;

- There is doubt as to whether the contractor

was at fault for the termination;

- There is doubt as to whether the default was beyond the control of and not caused by the negligence of the contractor;

- There is a disagreement over the meaning of various terms of the contract, which will need to be litigated;

- There is an assertion of government fault or negligence as a cause of the default;

- There is an assertion of government delay as a cause of negligence; or

- There is a question about the performance of a subcontractor or the direction of the CO with respect to the subcontractor.

81

You failed either to submit your termination for convenience settlement proposal within the one-year deadline, or to obtain a written extension from the contracting officer.

The government may terminate a contract for convenience, in whole or in part, if a CO determines that a termination is in the government's interest.[31] Termination is effected by delivering to the contractor a notice of termination specifying the extent of the termination and the effective date. Generally, the contractor is entitled to the contract price for all goods delivered and accepted, and to its costs, and a reasonable profit thereon, for any undelivered goods. A contractor who delays in filing a termination for convenience settlement proposal more than a year after the effective date of the termination runs a distinct risk of forfeiting money to which it was entitled. FAR 52.249-2 (e) states:

The contractor has one year from the effective date of the termination to submit a final settlement proposal to the contracting officer, unless the period is extended in writing by the contracting officer. If for some reason a termination proposal is not filed, the [c]ontracting [o]fficer may determine that if the facts justify it, a termination settlement proposal may be received and acted on after one year or any extension. If the [c]ontractor fails to submit the proposal within the time allowed, the [c]ontracting [o]fficer may determine, on the basis of information available, the amount, if any, due the [c]ontractor because of the termination and shall pay the amount determined.[32]

In practice, COs usually insist on receipt of a proper termination settlement within the one-year time period, or within a timeframe provided in a written extension. The one-year period for the submission of termination settlement proposals required by FAR 52.249(e) has been held enforceable by the government to effect a waiver of a contractor's right to a termination for convenience settlement.[33] Contractors are well-advised to submit a timely convenience settlement proposal within one year of the termination's effective date and to avoid this possibility of forfeiture.

82

In a termination for convenience settlement, you (or the auditor) rigidly applied the cost principles of FAR Part 31 instead of seeking a reasonable and fair settlement.

The courts and boards have made it very clear that if a contract is terminated for convenience, a settlement agreement must be fair and may not be based on any rigid principles in the *FAR*. FAR 49.201 states:

A settlement should compensate the contractor fairly for the work done and the preparations made for the terminated portions of the contract, including a reasonable allowance for profit. Fair compensation is a matter of judgment and cannot be measured exactly. In a given case, various methods may be equally appropriate for arriving at fair compensation. The use of business judgment, as distinguished from strict accounting principles, is the heart of a settlement… Cost and accounting data may provide guides, but are not rigid measures for ascertaining fair compensation.

FAR 49.113 continues this sentiment, expressing that "[t]he cost principles and procedures in the applicable subpart of Part 31 shall, subject to the general principles in [FAR] 49.201, be used in asserting, negotiating, or determining costs relevant to termination settlements…"

The courts have specifically endorsed this notion of fairness, notwithstanding the rules in FAR Part 31. In *Nicon, Inc., v. United States*,[34] the court held that the "overall purpose of a termination for convenience settlement is to fairly compensate the contractor and to make the contractor whole for the costs incurred in connection with the terminated work. The cost principles in Part 31.2…are…subject to the general fairness principles of [FAR] 49.201(a)."

An even clearer example is provided in the following passage from *McDonnell Douglas Corp. v. United States*,[35] which described the "tension between FAR Part 31 and Part 49":

[The government] argued that FAR Part 31 should be the focal point of the court's analysis; plaintiffs emphasized FAR Part 49…Part 31 generally may be described as establishing a formulaic, accounting-based structure, while Part 49 provides an equity-based framework. Because Part 31 is subject to the general principles of 49.201, we do not apply strict cost accounting principles here…We cannot ignore equitable considerations and reasonable business judgment in our deliberations.

Insist that any settlement agreement be fair and reasonable, or appeal the CO's final decision on your settlement proposal.

83

You failed to assert that any liquidated damages assessed against you bore no relation to the actual government costs (i.e., were punitive) and therefore, were invalid.

Liquidated damages are an amount established at contract award that sets forth the amount to be paid in the event of a breach. The use of a liquidated damages clause saves the time and expense of litigating the actual damages. However, liquidated damages must not be punitive and must be proportionate to the damages incurred.

Liquidated damages are frequently used where there is a delay in completion of a government construction contract or in the delivery of a government supply contract. The contract may specify a dollar amount to be forfeited by the contractor for each day or week of nondelivery. The *FAR* states that "[l]iquidated damages are not punitive and are not negative performance incentives. Liquidated damages are used to compensate the [g]overnment for probable damages. Therefore, the liquidated damages rate must be a reasonable forecast of just compensation for the harm that is caused by late delivery or untimely performance of the particular contract."[36]

In *Orbas & Associates*,[37] the Armed Services Board stated that liquidated damages will be enforced if they:

> are fair and reasonable attempts to fix just
> compensation for anticipated loss caused by delay
> in completion and, as of the time of making the

contract, actual damages are uncertain in nature and amount or are unmeasurable and the amount of damages stipulated is reasonable (i.e., bears a reasonable relationship to the anticipated loss). Conversely, a liquidated damages provision bearing no reasonable relationship to anticipated damages or greatly disproportionate to the presumed loss will be stricken entirely as an unenforceable penalty.

A party challenging a liquidated damages clause bears the burden of proving the clause unenforceable.[38] These are some examples of cases where liquidated damages clauses have been held unenforceable:

The government knew there would be no damages or additional cost—In a contract for interior painting, the government assessed $5,000 in liquidated damages for late performance. The liquidated damages clause was intended to capture the cost of the extra government supervision and inspection for each additional day of painting. However, the government knew there would be no concurrent daily inspection or superintendence costs at all in the event of delay. Therefore, the $100 per day was deemed a penalty and unenforceable.[39]

Liquidated damages were disproportionate to the loss or injury—In a contract for the installation of windows in on-base military housing, the setting of liquidated damage rates was based on the additional cost of off-base quartering residents beyond the deadline for performance. However, neither party contemplated that the residents would be forced to vacate the premises, and, in fact, no displacement of residents did occur. Because this was the case, the setting of liquidated damages rates based on quarters allowances (as if the premises would be vacated) was invalid.[40]

ENDNOTES

1. FAR 52.249-8.

2. FAR 49.607.

3. FAR 49.607.

4. "If, after termination [for default], it is determined that the [c]ontractor was not in default, or that the default was excusable, the rights and obligations of the parties shall be the same as if the termination had been issued for the convenience of the [g]overnment." FAR 52.249-8(g).

5. FAR 52.249-8.

6. Id.

7. *George A. Fuller Co. v. United States*, 69 F.Supp. 409, 415 (Ct. Cl. 1947).

8. *Kehm Corp. v. United States*, 93 F.Supp. 620, 623 (Ct. Cl. 1950).

9. FAR 52.249-8(f).

10. FAR 52.249-8(b).

11. FAR 9.104-1.

12. FAR 52.209-5 (a)(1)(ii), Certification Regarding Debarment, Suspension, Proposed Debarment, and Other Responsibility Matters.

13. FAR 9.104-3(b).

14. FAR 15.304(c)(3).

15. FAR 1.102-2.

16. FAR 15.305.

17. FAR 52.249-8(a)(1)(ii).

18. *Discount Co. v. United States*, 554 F.2d 435, 441 (Ct. Cl. 1977).

19. *State of Fla., Dept. of Ins., v. U.S.*, 33 Fed. Cl. 188 (1995).

20. *K & M Const.*, ENGBCA No. 2998, 72-1 B.C.A. ¶ 9,366.

21. ASBCA No. 48060, 06-2 BCA ¶ 33,316.

22. Id.

23. Id.

24. FAR 49.502.

25. *Cascade Pac. Int'l. v. United States*, 773 F.2d 287, 293-4 (Fed. Cir. 1985) (internal citations omitted).

26. *Astro-Space Labs., Inc., v. United States*, 470 F.2d 1003, 1018 (Ct. Cl. 1972).

27. Id.

28. GSBCA No. 6870, 85-3 BCA ¶ 18,376 (internal citations omitted).

29. FAR 49.402-4.

30. *McDonnell Douglas Corp. v. United States*, 323 F.3d 1006, 1015 (Fed. Cir. 2003).

31. FAR 52.249-2(a).

32. FAR 52.249-2(e); see also FAR. 49.206-1.

33. *Do-Well Machine Shop, Inc., v. United States*, 870 F.2d 637, 641 (Fed. Cir. 1989); see also *England v. Swanson Group*, 353 F.3d 1375 (Fed. Cir. 2004).

34. 331 F.3d 878, 885 (Fed. Cir. 2003).

35. 40 Fed. Cl. 529, 536 (1998) (internal citations omitted).

36. FAR 11.501(b).

37. ASBCA Nos. 32922, et al., 87-3 BCA ¶ 20,051 (internal citations omitted).

38. *DJ Mfg. Corp. v. United States*, 86 F.3d 1130, 1134 (Fed. Cir. 1996).

39. *Garden State Painting Co., Inc.*, ASBCA No. 22248, 78-2 BCA ¶ 13,499.

40. *Proserv, Inc.*, ASBCA No. 20768, 78-1 BCA ¶ 13,066.

Chapter 12

Audits

84

You failed to insist that auditors provide you with a specific request in writing from a contracting officer before providing access to your records.

Auditors, such as those from the Defense Contract Audit Agency (DCAA) or the inspector general (IG), do not have lawful authority to obtain or examine your company records without a specific request made by a contracting officer (CO) pertaining to a contract you have performed, you are currently performing, or on which you are submitting an offer. The authority to obtain records derives from various access-to-records clauses that are included in your contract. For example, FAR 52.215-2, Audit and Records–Negotiation, states:

> [T]he [c]ontractor shall maintain and the [c]ontracting [o]fficer, or an authorized representative of the [c]ontracting [o]fficer [such as an auditor], shall have the right to examine and audit all records and other evidence sufficient to reflect properly all costs claimed to have been incurred or anticipated to be incurred directly or indirectly in performance of this contract. This right of examination shall include inspection at all reasonable times of the [c]ontractor's plants, or parts of them, engaged in performing the contract.

Similarly, if the contractor has submitted cost or pricing data, "the [c]ontracting [o]fficer, or an authorized representative of the [c]ontracting [o]fficer," has the right to examine and audit the contractor's records "in order to evaluate the accuracy, completeness, and currency of the cost or pricing data."

There is a similar clause permitting access to the contractor's records by the Government Accountability Office (GAO)—headed by the comptroller general—which states that "[t]he [c]omptroller [g]eneral of the United States, or an authorized representative of the [c]omptroller [g]eneral, shall have access to and right to examine any of the [c]ontractor's directly pertinent records involving transactions related to this contract."[1]

The important point to note is that, without a written request from either a proper CO or the GAO, a contractor has no lawful obligation to permit access to its contract records. (Note: subpoenas or search warrants also provide lawful authority, but those will be discussed separately.) Because an auditor or the IG *wants* to examine your records does not mean that you *must* comply. An oral request to review your records is insufficient.

Not only should contractors insist that any audit be announced in writing, but contractors should also insist that they are afforded the full measure of protections embodied in *Government Auditing Standards,* including an overview of the objectives, scope, methodology, timing, and planned reporting of the audit before the audit is conducted—plus an exit briefing before the auditors leave the contractor's facility.[2]

85

You failed to insist that auditors provide you with a letter or entrance briefing explicitly stating the scope of the audit.

As noted in the previous mistake, auditors are required to communicate, before an audit, an overview of the objectives, scope, methodology, timing, and planned reporting of the audit.[3] This communication normally takes the form of a letter from the CO, but can also take place during the audit's entrance briefing. This pre-audit notice serves two objectives. First, it allows the contractor to begin gathering any relevant documents and helps expedite the audit. Second, and most important, it delineates the scope of the audit.

A contractor should cooperate in full with any audit and should provide any documents that fall within the audit's scope. However, if the audit's scope is not clearly delineated, an auditor may embark on the proverbial "fishing expedition," contrary to the policy underlying the auditing standards. Audits are designed to target specific contracts and specific issues. Fishing expeditions waste both the government's and the contractor's time and resources. Moreover, contractor management will be caught off guard and will be unable to present management's views on the suddenly shifting target of the audit.

Insist on a clear and concise pre-audit notice. If the notice is unclear, or if the auditor strays from the audit's scope, contact an experienced government contracts attorney immediately.

86

You failed to appoint a single point of contact with the auditors through which all requests, documents, copies, and communication would pass, and who would be present at all employee interviews.

Just as the government normally appoints a single point of contact (sometimes called an "audit focal point") when it announces an audit, the contractor should appoint a single person, and should notify the government of its single point of contact to serve as a conduit for all government requests for documents, interrogatories, etc. This person should already be familiar with the underlying

contract and should be able to provide requested information (provided it is within the scope of the audit) quickly and efficiently. If you grant auditors an opportunity to interview or otherwise have access to your employees (e.g., for identification of documents), it is imperative that the single point of contact be present at all times. The contractor's point of contact will also note all documents and information that have been provided and can inform management of where the audit appears to be heading next. If the auditors begin to stray outside the audit's scope, the point of contact can notify management immediately.

The need for a single point of contact for an audit cannot be stressed enough. Management needs to know what has passed through the auditors' hands and whom the auditors have spoken to so it will know how to respond. If an auditor requests and mistakenly receives inaccurate or irrelevant documents or information, the auditor's subsequent final conclusions and recommendations may be wildly off base and harmful to the company.

87

You allowed the auditors access to your employees other than for floor checks of timecards.

As noted earlier, the authority to obtain contractor records derives from various access-to-records clauses that are included in your contract. FAR 52.215-2, Audit and Records—Negotiation, states that the CO or an authorized representative of the CO may examine and audit all records that relate to the contract. The access to your records granted to the comptroller general of the GAO is similar: "access to and right to examine any of the [c]ontractor's directly pertinent records involving transactions related to this contract."[4] Nothing in any of the contract clauses permits an auditor or other government representative to interview or question your employees.

Over the years, auditors have been permitted limited access to employees as part of timecard audits. These interviews are often referred to as "floor checks," where an auditor ventures out onto the manufacturing floor and questions contractor employees with their timecards in hand. Auditors are permitted to inquire about contracts or programs that employees were or are currently working on, and that are reflected in the record of their timecards. This accommodation is made by contractors and permits auditors to stretch the access-to-records clause.

Auditors should not be given day-to-day access to your employees, such as in lunchrooms, at water fountains, or copying machines. Auditors will inevitably ask questions and may obtain information that is outside the audit's scope or that exceeds that found in the provided documents. The best advice is to place auditors in a single room and to have your point of contact shuttle documents to and from the room as requested by the auditors. This way, the auditors will be confined to the audit's proper scope and the point of contact can keep track of the documents and information provided.

If the auditor does embark on floor checks, make sure your point of contact is present and is aware of the proper scope of questioning—namely, timecards only. Refusing to grant auditors access to employees for floor checks altogether may be counterproductive. If access to employees for timecards is not granted, the suspicious auditor could refer the case to the IG, in which case a special agent or investigator could lawfully seek to question the employee.

88

You failed to insist that the auditors provide you with an exit briefing stating their findings.

The GAO yellow book requires that government auditors obtain the views of responsible contractor officials by providing with the auditor's draft findings in what is generally known as an exit briefing before the auditors leave the contractor's facility. This draft of the auditor's findings allows the contractor to provide the auditors with comments and helps ensure that the final report is fair, complete, and objective.[5]

Contractors should not forgo their right to an exit briefing. The contractor's single point of contact should know when the audit is at or near its conclusion, and should specifically request (or demand if need be) an exit briefing. If auditors refuse to provide an exit briefing for any reason, the contractor should contact the auditor's supervisor with the yellow book citation outlining the requirement in hand.

If the company does not receive an audit debriefing, it could be blindsided by the audit's final findings and recommendations. For example, if defective pricing is alleged, the company has a right to know the reasons and the estimated dollar impact at the time the auditor leaves. This knowledge gives management the chance to comment on the audit immediately and to research and recheck the auditor's facts. In either event, the contractor will be better prepared to discuss the matter later with the CO.

89

You failed to fully cooperate with an audit to the extent required by regulation.

Contractors have a lawful duty to cooperate with all lawful audits. Such cooperation extends to providing and disclosing all relevant documents that are within the scope of the audit and the auditors' proper requests. To fully cooperate, however, a contractor need not do the following:

- Permit its employees to be questioned or interviewed, except for floor checks.

- Perform data manipulation for the benefit of the auditor. For example, the auditor may ask the contractor to prepare a spreadsheet showing allocable costs by month. Your obligation extends only to giving auditors the records reflecting allocable costs per month. Auditors can create their own spreadsheets to examine and analyze the data.

- Provide access to documents or records that are not within the scope of audit. Only documents within the audit scope must be provided. If the audit's scope is formally changed, then more documents may be required.

Failure to cooperate can result in a re-audit, the withholding of funds, or, in the worst-case scenario, referral by the auditors to the IG for a criminal investigation. Criminal investigators do not politely ask for documents—they demand them through the use of subpoenas and, if necessary, the execution of search warrants. Criminal investigations are extremely difficult for a company and can result in criminal charges. Full cooperation with auditors, as previously mentioned, may make referral for a criminal investigation unnecessary.

ENDNOTES

1. FAR 52.215-2(d) and FAR 52.212-5(d) (for commercial contracts).

2. *Government Auditing Standards* (2007), GAO-07-162G, (often referred to as the "GAO yellow book" because of its color) §7.46.

3. *Government Auditing Standards* §7.46.

4. FAR 52.215-2(d) and FAR 52.212-5(d) (for commercial contracts).

5. Id. § 8.32.

Chapter 13

Integrity and Investigations

90

You failed to have a company compliance program in place— including a training program— outlining the company's procedures in the event of a criminal investigation.

Company compliance programs for government contractors can pay significant dividends. They will prevent most criminal wrongdoing by staff members. In the event that criminal wrongdoing does occur, they are likely to detect a problem early enough for the company to take corrective action, and to notify the appropriate authorities if necessary. In general, you should emphasize the following two rules of thumb:

- Be scrupulously honest in all dealings with the government, written or oral; and

- Provide only accurate statements, written or oral, to the government. In the event you discover that you've made an inaccurate statement, correct it immediately by informing the government of the error.

In addition to helping a contractor avoid criminal liability, compliance programs will also help prevent a contractor from making other costly mistakes such as:

- Failing to disclose all of a company's commercial sales practices and discounts when forming multiple award schedule (MAS) contracts;

- Failing to implement the required price reductions associated with most-favored-customer pricing on MAS contracts;

- Defectively pricing a contract proposal (i.e., submitting cost or pricing data to the government that is not current, accurate, and complete);

- Charging for unallowable items in invoices submitted to the government;

- Failing to pay minimum wages as required by Labor Department wage determinations;

- Failing to comply with the Buy American Act (BAA) or Trade Agreements Act clauses (TAA);

- Failing to comply with the Procurement Integrity Act;

- Violating subcontracting requirements;

- Improperly completing the representations and certifications in a bid or proposal;

- Failing to comply with equal opportunity and affirmative action requirements;

- Failing to comply with the rules on government furnished property; or

- Failing to comply with quality control or quality assurance provisions of a contract.

Compliance programs are a prophylactic measure, informing employees as to what they can and cannot do and sensitizing the entire company to the need for integrity and ethics in government contracting. The nine essential elements in an effective government contracts compliance program include:

1. A responsible individual to manage the program;

2. An ethics code;

3. Regular training and communication to employees;

4. A hotline;

5. Internal reviews;

6. Timely corrective actions;

7. A disciplinary mechanism or other means of enforcement;

8. Good discretion in delegation of authority; and

9. Self-reporting, cooperation, and acceptance of responsibility.[1]

91

You failed to appreciate the consequences of civil and criminal misconduct.

When compliance programs break down or are absent, government contractors will most likely run afoul of the criminal and civil laws in the following six areas:

1. **Criminal false statements**[2]—knowingly and willfully falsifying, concealing, or covering up a material fact by any trick, scheme, or device, or making or using any false, fictitious, or fraudulent statement, representation, writing or document in any matter within the jurisdiction of any U.S. government agency. Penalties include imprisonment for up to five years and a fine of up to $250,000 for each false statement.[3]

2. **Mail and wire fraud**[4]—using the mail or the wires, radio, or TV to execute a scheme or artifice to defraud or to obtain money or property by means of false or fraudulent pretenses. Penalties include imprisonment for up to five years and a fine of up to $250,000 for each fraudulent use of the mail or wires.

3. **Conspiracy**[5]—having two or more persons who conspire to commit any offense against the United States or to defraud the United States in any manner where one person takes at least one overt act in furtherance of the conspiracy. Penalties include imprisonment for up to five years and a fine of up to $250,000.

4. **Obstruction**[6]—obstructing or endeavoring to obstruct or impede the due administration of justice or administration of federal law. Penalties include imprisonment for up to 10 years and a fine of up to $250,000.

5. **Criminal false claims**[7]—making or presenting to the U.S. government any claim against the United States, knowing such claim to be false, fictitious, or fraudulent. Proof beyond a reasonable doubt is required. Penalties include imprisonment for up to five years and a fine of up to $250,000 for each false claim.

6. **Civil false claims**[8]—knowingly presenting to the U.S. government a false or fraudulent claim for payment. Proof by a preponderance of the evidence is required—a lesser standard than the proof beyond a reasonable doubt needed to prove a criminal false claim. Penalties for each false claim include a fine of between $5,000 and $10,000 plus three times the amount of loss sustained by the government. Civil false claim actions often follow a criminal false statement or false claims conviction and thereby substantially increase the penalties.

The major difference between a civil false claim and a criminal one is the standard of proof—proof beyond a reasonable doubt to establish a criminal false claim and proof by a preponderance of the evidence for civil false claims—and the fact that civil false claims encompass additional acts beyond the mere submission of a request for money (i.e., being part of a conspiracy, creating a false record, creating a false receipt, delivering less property than required, etc.).

The consequences flowing from the commission of any one of the earlier-described acts are numerous and significant. The costs of defending a criminal or civil action alone should deter a would-be overzealous or cheating contractor from such conduct. Contractors must establish an effective compliance program that trains employees and emphasizes the importance of accurate statements in all aspects of government contracting as discussed above.[9] Lack of institutional control is not a defense.

92

You failed to inform your employees of their rights and obligations during an investigation.

The general approach of criminal investigators, such as the Federal Bureau of Investigation (FBI) or an agency's inspector general, is to obtain documents through subpoena, search warrant, or voluntary surrender by employees; then to interview employees in a tough fashion to elicit an acknowledgment of wrongdoing. The investigators then use those admissions to work up the chain to the higher echelons of corporate management. If employees do not submit to questioning, investigators can work through a United States attorney to compel their answers through subpoenas. Unfortunately, the glare on an investigation can lead to some seemingly bizarre employee behavior, including confessions for acts that the employee had absolutely nothing to do with. During an investigation, employees should be notified of the following:

- Employees have the right to refuse an interview by an investigator. This right is

particularly important because investigators usually confront the employee at times and places where company counsel cannot be easily contacted.

- Employees have the right to insist that company counsel or counsel of their own choosing be present at any investigative interview.

- Any answers given to an investigator must be truthful. Any false statements given to investigators are potentially separate criminal offenses.

Normally, this advice is given to employees in annual compliance training and in the company's ethics program. But if an investigation begins, company counsel should immediately prepare a memorandum for all employees explaining their rights. The company should volunteer to have corporate counsel attend any interviews, which should prevent any strong-arm tactics by investigators and should provide the company with a better understanding of where the investigation is heading.

93

You failed to inform your employees that all company documents belong to the company.

A compliance program must explain that company documents belong to the company and not to the person who happens to currently possess the documents. Employees commonly confuse physical custody with ownership. They sometimes may take home documents, but the company still owns them. Every company should have a written policy and set of procedures relating to the release of company documents to avoid inadvertent disclosure, particularly of privileged documents. Any document release should be routed through and approved by the contractor's general counsel or another appropriate company official.

94

You ignored a conflict of interest.

FAR 3.101-1 states:

> Government business shall be conducted in a manner above reproach and…with complete impartiality and with preferential treatment for none. Transactions relating to the expenditure of public funds require the highest degree of public trust and an impeccable standard of conduct. The general rule is to avoid strictly any conflict of interest or even the appearance of a conflict of interest in [g]overnment-contractor relationships. While many [f]ederal laws and regulations place restrictions on the actions of [g]overnment personnel, their official conduct must, in addition, be such that they would have no reluctance to make a full public disclosure of their actions.

The Supreme Court has noted that conflict of interest rules, like FAR 3.101-1 above, are "directed at an evil which endangers the very fabric of a democratic society, for a democracy is only effective if the people have faith in those who govern, and that faith is bound to be shattered when high officials and their appointees engage in activities which arouse suspicions or malfeasance and corruption."[10]

Breaches of the standard of conduct described in FAR 3.101-1 and the public trust can have grave consequences for contractors that find themselves embroiled in such affairs. Consider the scandal outlined in *Lockheed Martin Corp.*[11] and *Lockheed Martin Aeronautics Co.*[12] Both of these protests were brought by Lockheed Martin, which lost two major defense contracts to Boeing. The protests were

based on admissions arising from the criminal conviction of Darleen Druyun, the Air Force's principal deputy assistant secretary for acquisition. Specifically, she acknowledged that Boeing's employment of her daughter and future son-in-law, at her request, along with her own desire to be employed by Boeing, influenced her decision-making in matters affecting Boeing.

Boeing's senior vice president and general counsel, Doug Bain, related in a January 2006 speech that, in one of the disputed procurements, Boeing acquired 25,000 pages of documents, many of which bore the proprietary markings of Lockheed Martin. When an employee came forward and brought the documents to management's attention, Boeing investigated, but "did a poor job on the investigation…[and] a poor job disclosing it to the government." The senior vice president and general counsel rhetorically asked, "What was the internal control system for the bidding practices… Where was management throughout this?"[13]

When the dust settled, Druyun and Boeing's chief financial officer, Mike Sears, were convicted of violations of federal conflict of interest laws and were sentenced to prison. In 2006, Boeing agreed to pay a record $615 million in settlement, which included a penalty of $50 million. The public relations hit that Boeing took was incalculable.

You should establish internal controls within your organization with an eye toward identifying and eliminating potential conflicts of interest. If you find yourself entangled in a conflict of interest situation, do not look the other way. Contact government contract counsel immediately and prepare to divulge all relevant information to the government.

ENDNOTES

1. See, generally, U.S.S.G. § 8B2.1.

2. 18 U.S.C. § 1001.

3. Sentence of fine, 18 U.S.C. § 3571.

4. 18 U.S.C. § 1341, and § 1343.

5. 18 U.S.C. § 371.

6. 18 U.S.C. § 1503 and § 1505.

7. 18 U.S.C. § 287.

8. 31 U.S.C. § 3729.

9. The attributes of an effective government contract compliance program were explained in a July 1999 article by Richard D. Lieberman, "Compliance Programs: They're Worth It!" *Contract Management* (Vol. 39, No. 7).

10. *United States v. Mississippi Valley Generating Co.*, 364 U.S. 520, 562 (1961).

11. B-295402, Feb. 18, 2005, 2005 CPD ¶ 24.

12. B-295401, Feb. 24, 2005, 2005 WL 502840.

13. Speech by Doug Bain at Boeing Leadership Meeting on January 5, 2006, in Orlando, Florida, reprinted in *Seattle Times*, January 31, 2006.

Chapter 14

Contract Disputes

95

You failed to include a sum certain in your claim.

To submit a proper claim for monetary relief in accordance with the FAR and the Contract Disputes Act of 1978 (CDA), a contractor must submit the claim in writing to the contracting officer (CO); the claim must request a final decision (no magic words needed); and, if the claim is for more than $100,000, the claim must be certified by an appropriate contractor official. In addition, the claim must include a sum certain.

A statement that you are owed "no less than" or "in excess of" some stated dollar amount is insufficient to meet the CDA's requirement of a sum certain. In a case before the Armed Services Board, a contractor submitted an appeal based on a claim asking for "no less than $1,072,957.05, plus all additional days of delay at $3,612.65 per day until the date of termination."[1] The board was forced to dismiss the appeal on jurisdictional grounds, stating:

> No matter what certainty might be present in the calculation of the $1,072,957.05 amount, or in the calculation of an amount for the additional days of delay, [the contractor's] claim letter qualified those amounts by the phrase "no less than"....[A] "not less than" amount is not a sum certain for purposes of the CDA[,] [n]or is it distinguishable from an "in excess of" amount which we have also held not to be a sum certain for purposes of the CDA.[2]

The lesson: If you are submitting a claim for monetary relief, state an unqualified amount that you are owed as a matter of right. If the amount owed is increasing by the day, state a sum certain that you are owed on the date of filing. Then give an unqualified amount that you are owed for each subsequent day, week, month, or year.

96

You failed to request an equitable adjustment when warranted.

Under the FAR, contractors are eligible for numerous different equitable adjustments arising out of the performance of their contracts and the actions of the government. It is generally advisable to assert your right to an equitable adjustment wherever permitted. When you submit your request for an equitable adjustment, you must comply with the requirements in both the FAR and in your contract.

Here are some specific examples of clear-cut situations enumerated in the FAR where an equitable adjustment is prescribed:

- Contract modifications that result from either unilateral or bilateral changes.[3]

- Failure to provide timely disposition instructions for disposal of inventory.[4]

- Under the termination clause, after partial termination, adjustment in the price or prices of the continued portion of a fixed-price contract.[5]

- If the security classification or security requirements of a contract are changed by the government.[6]

- If there is a variation in estimated quantity and the quantity of a unit-priced item in a contract is an estimated quantity and the actual quantity of the unit-priced item varies more than 15 percent above or below the prescribed quantity.[7]

- If the contractor is requested by the CO to revise technical data to reflect engineering design changes made during the performance of a contract and affecting the form, fit, and function of any item (other than technical data) delivered under the contract.[8]

- If the contract cost is affected by a change that the contractor is required to make to the contractor's established cost accounting practices.[9]

- If the CO issues a stop work order which he or she subsequently cancels (such as in the case of a bid protest).[10]

- If the contractor encounters materially different site conditions that cause an increase or decrease in the contractor's cost of, or the time required for, performing any part of the work under the contract.[11]

- If the performance of all or any part of the work is, for an unreasonable period of time, suspended, delayed, or interrupted by the government (including failure to act in a reasonable time).[12]

- Any constructive change (i.e., an actual change without a change order).[13]

- If government furnished property is not delivered to the contractor on time, or if the property is delivered in a condition not suitable for its intended use.[14]

Contractors should cite these regulations when the situations arise and when they are entitled to an equitable adjustment. Note that the earlier list is neither exhaustive nor exclusive. An equitable adjustment may be owed in any number of situations where the government is responsible for an increase in the contractor's costs.

97

After you realized your equitable adjustment would not be honored by the contracting officer, you failed to submit a proper claim.

Contractors must diligently submit requests for equitable adjustment (REAs) when they are so entitled. Unfortunately, nothing in the *FAR* requires the CO to act on an REA within a particular time frame. For example, the changes clause merely states that if a change ordered by the CO "causes an increase or decrease in the cost of, or the time required for, performance of any part of the work under this contract, whether or not changed by the order, the [c]ontracting [o]fficer shall make an equitable adjustment in the contract price, the delivery schedule, or both, and shall modify the contract."[15] It should be noted that, there is no time limit provided for the CO to make a decision on the equitable adjustment or issue the required modification. Therefore, contractors must follow up on their REAs, converting them into formal claims when necessary.

A contractor's REA should include a specific and reasonable time frame for a decision by the CO. Typically, 30 days is sufficient for smaller claims, while a longer period is more appropriate for complex claims. Regardless of the time frame selected, the contractor should make it clear that if the CO ignores the REA, the contractor will consider the matter in dispute and submit a claim. Only a formal claim will trigger the disputes process, thus providing the contractor with the opportunity to seek redress at a board or the U.S. Court of Federal Claims (COFC).

A claim, as defined in the disputes clause and the CDA, is "a written demand or written assertion by one of the contracting parties seeking, as a matter of right, the payment of money in a sum certain, the adjustment or interpretation of contract terms, or other relief arising under or relating to [the] contract."[16] Additionally, claims of more than $100,000 must be certified. The required certification is as follows:

> I certify that the claim is made in good faith, that the supporting data are accurate and complete to the best of my knowledge and belief, that the amount requested accurately reflects the contract adjustment for which the contractor believes the [g]overnment is liable, and that I am duly authorized to certify the claim on behalf of the [c]ontractor.[17]

The certification must be executed by a person duly authorized to bind the contractor with respect to a claim (i.e., someone who is authorized to sign contracts or modifications on behalf of the contractor).

The claim must be provided to the CO in writing and must be summarized with sufficient specificity that the CO will understand what is in dispute. To the maximum extent possible, the summary should do the following:

- Discuss the relevant contract requirements;

- Explain the actual work performed or how the work was impeded;

- Outline the increased costs or delay forming the basis of the claim;

- Show how the sum claimed was calculated;

- Provide the legal basis or theory of recovery forming the basis of the claim;

- Request a final decision from the CO;

- Seek payment as a matter of right;

- Seek a sum certain (an exact amount);

- Be nonroutine (in dispute) (i.e., not be an invoice, voucher, or routine request for payment); and

- Be certified if more than $100,000.

Although not required, a contractor should obtain proof of the claim's receipt. If the claim has been submitted properly, the CO must rule on it, or it will be deemed denied after 60 days.

98

When the contracting officer failed to issue a final decision on your claim within 60 days of its submission (or failed to schedule a date certain for issuance of a final decision), you failed to deem your claim denied and to immediately appeal to a board of contract appeals or the U.S. Court of Federal Claims.

It is human nature to delay difficult decisions, and COs are human beings. However, contractors should not let this prevent them from obtaining a resolution of their important claims.

Frequently, COs either fail to make a final decision on a claim in a timely manner or ignore the claim altogether. Fortunately, the CDA provides an escape hatch for the contractor. Under the CDA, a CO must issue a decision on any claim of $100,000 or less within 60 days. For claims of more than $100,000, the CO must either issue a decision within 60 days of receipt or notify the contractor of the time within which a decision will be issued (which has been interpreted to mean an exact number of days or an exact date[18]). Most importantly, the CDA provides that "[a]ny failure by the contracting officer to issue a decision…within the period required will be deemed to be a decision by the contracting officer denying the claim and will authorize the commencement of the appeal or suit on the claim [in the COFC or a board]."[19]

This deemed denied provision gives contractors a simple remedy for recalcitrant COs who fail to comply with the CDA's final decision requirements. Contractors can immediately file an appeal of their claim at the board or the COFC, and either will acknowledge jurisdiction. The court or board may either commence the appeal or stay proceedings and order the CO to make a final decision.[20] The only reason for not proceeding with a deemed denial on a claim would be if the contractor was engaged in delicate negotiations with a CO that would be upset by the initiation of an appeal.

99

You selected the wrong forum for your appeal.

After you have decided to file an appeal of a CO's final decision on your claim, it is important to select the right forum. The CDA provides two alternate forums for challenging the decision—a contractor may file at the appropriate board of contract appeals[21] or the COFC.[22] The initial forum selection is important because the CDA has been interpreted as precluding contractors from pursuing a claim in both forums[23] (i.e., once a contractor makes its choice, it's stuck with that choice and may no longer pursue its claim in the alternate forum).

There are two boards of contract appeals, the Armed Services Board of Contract Appeals (ASBCA), which generally handles appeals of military contracts, and the Civilian Board of Contract Appeals (CBCA), which handles everything else. The purpose of the boards is "to

provide a swift, inexpensive method of resolving contract disputes."[24] As such, they provide accelerated procedures for smaller claims. In general, compared to the COFC, the boards have simpler procedural rules. Board judges are appointed through regular civil service procedures that are based on merit and experience.

The COFC is a much more formal forum with rules similar to a U.S. District Court. Judges in the COFC are appointed by the president and confirmed by the U.S. Senate. Unlike the boards, the COFC has no special accelerated or small claims procedures. Some other differences include the following:

- An officer of a corporation may represent that party before a board; only an attorney may represent a corporation at the COFC.

- All that is needed to appeal a decision to a board is a simple one-page notice (a complaint is required 30 days later); at the COFC, a complaint is required at the outset.

- At the boards, agencies must provide all relevant documents in their possession in a contract appeal file; formal discovery requests are required at the COFC.

- At the boards, small claims procedures provide for resolution of the appeal within 120 days of docketing, where the amount in dispute is $50,000 or less ($150,000 or less if the appellant is a small business concern). No such small claims procedures are used at the COFC.

- At the boards, accelerated procedures provide for resolution of the appeal within 180 days of docketing, where the amount in dispute is $100,000 or less. There is no such procedure at the COFC.

- Conference calls between the parties and the judge to simplify and expedite proceedings are typical at the boards. Although this arrangement may be available on occasion at the COFC, it is unusual.

Some similarities include:

- Full scope of discovery in board and COFC rules,

- Provisions for alternative dispute resolution at both the boards and COFC, and

- Reimbursement of litigation expenses under the Equal Access to Justice Act available in both forums.

Many forum decisions are based on the amount of time that has passed since the CO issued a final decision on the contractor's claim. Contractors have 90 days to appeal to a board and 12 months to appeal to the COFC. Thus, if a contractor waits longer than 90 days, the only forum remaining is the COFC.

The availability of accelerated and small claims procedures at the boards is an important difference, because it gives the contractor a relatively quick and inexpensive means of redress from an unfavorable decision by a CO. Election of these expedited procedures has the added benefit of placing pressure on an agency to settle outside of the boards as a result of time constraints.

On balance, it is probably best to bring smaller dollar value appeals to the boards and, if appropriate, to use the small claims or accelerated procedures to speed up the process. Typically, an appeal under $100,000 should not be brought before the COFC unless, as noted earlier, 90 days have already passed since the CO's final decision. There are certain types of appeals where the boards have developed a special expertise, such as defective pricing, and even large dollar value cases in this area may be better brought to the boards rather than to the COFC. No matter

the choice, the contractor will receive fair treatment from outstanding, well-qualified judges. And finally, if dissatisfied with the results in either forum, the contractor may bring an appeal to the Court of Appeals for the Federal Circuit.

ENDNOTES

1. *Sandoval Plumbing Repair, Inc.*, ASBCA No. 54640, 05-2 BCA ¶ 33072.

2. Id.

3. FAR 43.103.

4. FAR 45.602-1.

5. FAR 49.208.

6. FAR 52.204-2.

7. FAR 52.211-18.

8. FAR 52.227-21.

9. FAR 52.230-2.

10. FAR 52.233-3.

11. FAR 52.236-2.

12. FAR 52.242-14.

13. FAR 52.243-1 (fixed price changes and other change order clauses).

14. FAR 52.245-1.

15. FAR 52.243-1.

16. FAR 52.233-1.

17. FAR 33.207.

18. *McDonnell Douglas Corp.*, ASBCA No. 48432, 96-1 BCA ¶ 28166 (contracting officer must pinpoint a particular date for final decision on claim).

19. 41 U.S.C. § 605(c).

20. 41 U.S.C. § 605(c)(5).

21. 41 U.S.C. § 606.

22. 41 U.S.C. § 609(a)(1).

23. See *Nat'l Neighbors, Inc., v. United States*, 839 F.2d 1539, 1542 (Fed. Cir. 1988).

24. *Dewey Electronics Corp. v. United States*, 803 F.2d 650, 655 (Fed. Cir. 1986).

Chapter 15

Performance Quality

100

You failed to perform as a world-class contractor.

In today's government contracting environment, satisfactory performance will not ensure current or future success. For the contractor to grow as a business, the performance of a government contractor must be world-class and must demonstrate that the contractor shares the concerns of its agency client. Here are some suggestions that may help make you a world-class contractor:

- Provide effective and efficient solutions to your customer's problems.

- Be innovative when problems arise.

- Recommend improvements and efficiencies for contract processes and procedures; for example, recommend appropriate value engineering change proposals (suggestions made by the contractor for performing the contract more economically).

- Provide superior service to your government customer.

- Provide a skilled, well-trained, capable, and professional contract workforce.

Glossary of Key Terms and Acronyms

AAFES	Army and Air Force Exchange Service
ACO	administrative contracting officer
ASBCA	Armed Services Board of Contract Appeals
BAA	Buy American Act
BAFO	best and final offer
CBA	collective bargaining agreement
CBCA	Civilian Board of Contract Appeals
CDA	Contract Disputes Act of 1978
CICA	Competition in Contracting Act of 1984 (the basic federal law designed to promote full and open competition in the award of government contracts)
change order	A written order (modification) signed by the CO, directing the contractor to make a change without the contractor's consent
claim	Written demand for payment or other relief stemming from a government contract and certified if the amount claimed is over $100,000
CO	contracting officer (a person with legal authority to bind the government on matters involving a particular contract)
COC	Certificate of Competency (issued by the Small Business Administration to denote that a small business is conclusively deemed responsible with respect to a particular procurement)
COFC	U.S. Court of Federal Claims
compensable delay	When a CO suspends, delays, or interrupts the performance of a contract for an unreasonable period of time
Contract Disputes Act	Comprehensive federal statute that establishes procedures for adjudicating government contract disputes
constructive change	When, by a COs act or omission or for other reasons, a contract is effectively modified, but without a written change order or modification

COR/COTR	contracting officer's representative/contracting officer's technical representative
cost-reimbursement contract	A contract in which the government agrees to pay "allowable" costs incurred by the contractor, plus some type of fee constituting the contractor's profit
CPAF	cost-plus-award-fee contract
CPIF	cost-plus-incentive-fee contract
CSP	commercial sales practices
cure notice	A notice that states a contractor is not in compliance with the terms of the contract or is endangering the contract's performance and grants the contractor 10 days to cure the problem
DARO	delivery after receipt of order
DCAA	Defense Contract Audit Agency
DCMA	Defense Contract Management Agency
debarment	An action excluding a contractor from government contracting and government-approved subcontracting for a specified period
DFARS	*Defense Federal Acquisition Regulation Supplement*
DO	debarment official
DOD	Department of Defense (includes Army, Navy, Air Force, Marine Corps, Defense Logistics Agency, and other defense agencies)
DSMD	discount schedule and marketing data
EFT	electronic funds transfer
EPA	economic price adjustment
equitable adjustment	Relief granted to a contractor, resulting from a change, constructive change, or compensable delay
ESLH	estimated standard labor hours

False Claims Act (Civil and Criminal)	Attaches civil or criminal liability to a party who knowingly presents either a false claim or a false record in support of a claim
FAR	*Federal Acquisition Regulation* (uniform, governmentwide set of regulations for all government contracting)
FBI	Federal Bureau of Investigation
fixed-price contract	A contract in which the government agrees at the time of the contract's award to pay a specific price for completed work and delivered products or services
FOIA	Freedom of Information Act
FPR	final proposal revision
GAO	Government Accountability Office (government agency, headed by the comptroller general of the United States, which renders opinions on disbursement of government funds, decides the merits of protests regarding contract awards, and analyzes government programs)
GFP	government furnished property
GPE	government point of entry
GSA	General Services Administration
HUBZone	historically underutilized business zone
ID/IQ	indefinite delivery/indefinite quantity
IFB	invitation for bids (a solicitation for a procurement using sealed bidding)
IG	inspector general
LOC	limitation of cost
LOF	limitation of funds
MAS	multiple award schedule contract
MOL	maximum ordering limitation

negotiated procurement	Contracting through the use of competitive proposals, optional discussions, and FPRs
OIG	Office of the Inspector General
PPA	Prompt Payment Act
protest	A written objection with regard to a solicitation submitted by an interested party who believes an agency has violated applicable procurement statutes and regulations.
REA	request for equitable adjustment
responsible contractor	A contractor capable of performing a contract that has a satisfactory record of integrity and performance
responsive bid	A bid that conforms with and commits to meet the material terms of an IFB
RFP	request for proposals (a solicitation for a negotiated procurement)
RFQ	request for quotations
SAT	simplified acquisition threshold
SBA	Small Business Administration
SCA	Service Contract Act
sealed bidding	Procurement by obtaining sealed bids and awarding the contract to the lowest priced responsible bidder whose bid is responsive
solicitation	An IFB or RFP
SOW	statement of work
TAA	Trade Agreements Act
termination for convenience	The right of the government to cancel a contract in whole or in part for any reason (absent bad faith), if the CO determines that it is in the best interest of the government

termination for default	The right of the government to cancel a contract in whole or in part, if a contractor fails to perform in accordance with the contract or endangers performance.
TIN	taxpayer identification number
TINA	Truth in Negotiation Act
UCC	Uniform Commercial Code

Index

Page references in bold denote abbreviations and term definitions.

About the Authors

Richard D. Lieberman is a partner in the law firm of McCarthy, Sweeney & Harkaway, P.C. He has been directly or indirectly involved in government contracts for his entire 39-year career and now concentrates exclusively on all aspects of federal procurement law. He served in the Office of the Secretary of Defense, on the staff of the U.S. Senate Appropriations Committee, and as assistant inspector general and deputy inspector general of the Department of Defense. Since 1988, he has been in the private practice of law and has concentrated on all aspects of contract formation, contract administration, debarment, audits, and investigations. He is the author or co-author of five books and numerous articles on government contracting. He received a J.D. from Georgetown University, an M.A. from the University of Wisconsin–Madison, and a B.A. from Cornell University.

Jason D. Morgan was introduced to federal procurement as a Navy Supply Corps officer aboard the fast-attack submarine USS *San Francisco*. In law school, he focused his studies on government contracts and worked alongside Richard Lieberman at McCarthy, Sweeney & Harkaway, P.C. Together, they co-authored an article, "The Basics of Government Contracts—A Primer," in *Contract Management* in August 2007. He holds a B.A. from the University of Florida and will graduate with a J.D. from George Washington University in May 2008. Upon graduation, he will join the Honorable Lawrence J. Block, judge of the U.S. Court of Federal Claims, for a two-year federal clerkship.